Reforming Non-Tariff Measures

DIRECTIONS IN DEVELOPMENT
Trade

Reforming Non-Tariff Measures

From Evidence to Policy Advice

Olivier Cadot, Michael J. Ferrantino, Julien Gourdon, and José-Daniel Reyes

WORLD BANK GROUP

Contents

Boxes

Figures

Tables

Acknowledgments

The team welcomes valuable guidance and support from Mona Haddad during the initial stages of this project and from Jose Reis, Caroline Freund, and Bill Maloney during its final stages. We received valuable peer review comments from Erhan Artuc, Julian Clarke, Lionel Fontagné, Ian Gillson, Mariem Malouche, and Michele Ruta. The patient and steady support of Mary Fisk in the World Bank Group's publications unit was essential to this task. Tanya Cubbins prepared the final, edited manuscript with grace and professionalism.

This work benefited from the support of the Multi-Donor Trust Fund for Trade and Development 2 financed by DFID (United Kingdom), SECO (Switzerland), SIDA (Sweden), the Netherlands Ministry of Foreign Affairs, the Norwegian Ministry of Foreign Affairs, Japan's Ministry of Finance, and the National Graduate Institute for Policy Studies.

About the Authors

Olivier Cadot holds a PhD in economics from Princeton University and an MA in economic history from McGill University. He is professor of international economics and director of the Institute of Applied Economics at the University of Lausanne. Formerly, he was associate professor of economics at INSEAD. He has held visiting appointments at the University of California at Los Angeles, McGill University, New York University, Université d'Auvergne, Koç University, and the Institut d'Etudes Politiques de Paris. He has been mission chief and consultant on World Bank missions to emerging countries and has advised the French government, the Swiss federal government, and the European Commission on trade policy matters. He also has worked for the Organisation for Economic Co-operation and Development (OECD) and the International Monetary Fund. He was elected best teacher of the year at the Faculty of Business and Economics at the University of Lausanne and was nominated three times for the Outstanding Teacher Award at INSEAD. He has contributed regularly to international executive programs.

Michael J. Ferrantino is lead economist and global product specialist for trade policy and integration at the World Bank. Prior to joining the World Bank, he served as lead international economist at the U.S. International Trade Commission from 1994 to 2013. His published research spans a wide array of topics relating to international trade, including non-tariff measures and trade facilitation; global value chains; relationship of trade to the environment, innovation, and productivity; and U.S.-China trade. He has taught at Southern Methodist, Youngstown State, Georgetown, American, and George Washington universities, and he has partnered on research projects with Asia-Pacific Economic Cooperation, OECD, the World Trade Organization, and the World Economic Forum. He holds a PhD in economics from Yale University.

Julien Gourdon has been an economist with the OECD since 2014. He specializes in international trade and development economics. His main topics of interest are trade policies, export competitiveness, trade and income inequality, and the impact evaluation of trade assistance projects. Formerly, he was an economist at the CEPII from 2011 to 2014 and at the World Bank from 2006 to 2011. He holds a PhD in economics from the University of Clermont Auvergne (CERDI).

José-Daniel Reyes is a senior economist in the Macroeconomics, Trade, and Investment Global Practice of the World Bank. He has more than 10 years of research and policy experience, working on issues of international trade, foreign direct investment, and globalization. Prior to joining the World Bank, he worked for the Inter-American Development Bank and for the Colombian government monitoring country performance in the Latin American region. He holds a PhD in economics from Georgetown University.

Abbreviations

ALADI	*Asociación Latinoamericana de Integración*
ASEAN	Association of Southeast Asian Nations
ATIGA	ASEAN Trade in Goods Agreement
AVE	ad valorem equivalent
CEPII	Centre d'Études Prospectives et d'Informations Internationales
CEPT	Common Effective Preferential Tariff
CO	certificate of origin
COFEMER	*Comisión Federal de Mejora Regulatoria*
COMESA	Common Market for Eastern and Southern Africa
CoRE NTM	Compilation of Reported NTMs
EAC	East African Community
EDD	Exporter Dynamics Database
EIU	Economist Intelligence Unit
EU	European Union
FDI	foreign direct investment
GDP	gross domestic product
HHS	household survey
HS	Harmonized System
IBP	international best practices
MAST	Multi-Agency Support Team
MoC	Ministry of Commerce
MRA	mutual recognition arrangement
NTB	non-tariff barrier
NTM	non-tariff measure
NTMC	NTM committee
OECD	Organisation for Economic Co-operation and Development
RTA	regional trade agreement
SMEs	small and medium enterprises
SPS	sanitary and phytosanitary

TBT	technical barriers to trade
TFA	Trade Facilitation Agreement
UDE	Economic Deregulation Unit
UNCTAD	United Nations Conference on Trade and Development
USTR	United States Trade Representative
WTO	World Trade Organization

Overview

The continued presence of non-tariff measures (NTMs) may be an important reason why trade costs remain stubbornly high, possibly creating a drag on economic growth. Countries that are more open to trade are more likely to experience strong growth performance. After decades of global tariff liberalization, trade costs continue to be high, particularly in low-income countries. Thus, the streamlining of NTMs can be an important part of country-level competitiveness agendas, even though there are other sources of high trade costs.

In reforming NTMs, it is important to recognize that they come in many different types and can be either welfare creating or welfare reducing. Although some are aimed purely at reducing trade and are likely to be welfare reducing, others emerge as the outcome of regulation of safety, health, or the environment and can in principle be welfare creating, but only if they are properly designed. There have been some regional efforts at tackling NTMs, for example, in the Association of Southeast Asian Nations and the Common Market for Eastern and Southern Africa. These efforts attempt to distinguish NTMs that may have a justified purpose from NTBs that have a primary effect of restricting trade. They may use either official data or private-sector complaints.

A variety of tools can be used to compare the prevalence of NTMs in one country as opposed to another. The inventory approach measures NTMs as a share, either of the total number of tariff lines for which there are imports *(frequency ratio)*, the total value of imports covered by NTMs *(coverage ratio)*, or the pervasiveness score, which takes into account the possibility that one product may face more than one NTM policy.

The actual market effect of NTMs may be calculated as an AVE (tariff equivalent). An AVE can be obtained using either price-based methods or quantity-based methods. *Handicraft methods* of calculating AVEs focus on one product at a time, taking into account the institutional details of a particular policy. *Mass-produced estimates* using econometric methods are useful for broad comparisons between countries and sectors, but they are less accurate at the level of individual products and policies. The *regulatory distance* approach allows assessment of whether a country's pattern of NTMs converge to or diverge from those of other countries. If a certain country or group of countries is taken to represent best practice, the regulatory distance approach yields normative as well as positive results.

The effects of NTMs on both consumers and producers can be addressed using quantitative methods. The impact of NTMs on poverty and income distribution operates through two different channels. NTMs that increase prices reduce the standard of living of consumers and potentially raise the incomes of producers in some sectors that are protected by NTMs. An analysis of sanitary and phytosanitary measures in Kenya show that their income-reducing effects are greater for poor consumers than for rich ones. NTMs are pervasive in markets for intermediate goods used in global value chains, such as in the apparel, footwear, electronics, and motor vehicle sectors.

In getting to policy advice, appropriate measurement tools need to be paired with a detailed institutional understanding of the operation of specific types of NTMs. This point is illustrated by four specific cases.

- In Indonesia, a registration requirement for standards on imported iron bars is shown to raise the cost of imports, having different effects on different trading partners.
- In Cambodia, registration requirements on exporters impose a fixed cost of exporting and adversely affect medium-sized exporters more than larger ones.
- In Nigeria, a long list of import prohibitions is estimated to raise consumer prices of the products imported by an average of 77 percent. Eliminating these prohibitions would raise an estimated 3.3 million Nigerians above the international poverty line and increase real national income by 8.5 percent.
- In Morocco, harmonization of NTMs with the European Union has offsetting negative and positive effects—imposing new costs on imports originating in low- and middle-income countries while encouraging new entry from imports originating in the European Union.

CHAPTER 1

Introduction

The empirical case for trade as an engine of growth has now been established on fairly solid empirical grounds. There has been a protracted controversy in the literature on the econometrics of trade and growth. Nonetheless, most recent estimates suggest that a major episode of liberalization provides a permanent boost in growth on the order of 1 to 2 percent.

Concomitantly, and largely on practical grounds, most low- and middle-income countries, with very few exceptions, have substantially lowered their trade barriers, eliminating the most egregious forms of trade protection (tariff peaks, quantitative restrictions, and other command-and-control instruments).

Yet, by all accounts, trade costs remain high. Using an approach that consists of inverting the gravity equation and inferring trade costs from the relative size of external versus internal trade, Arvis and others (2013) and Novy (2013) show that trade costs have failed to fall as much for low-income countries as they have for others, reinforcing their economic "remoteness."

Several multilateral initiatives have been set up to help low- and middle-income countries—in particular, low-income ones—to integrate better in world trade. For instance, the Aid-for-Trade initiative was launched in 2005 to help low-income countries to cope with their Uruguay Round commitments, which were, in turn, expected to improve their ability to draw benefits from World Trade Organization (WTO) membership.

More recently, the Trade Facilitation Agreement (TFA) signed in December 2013 in Bali and entered into force in February 2017, was designed to help low- and middle-income countries to focus on reducing non-tariff barriers (NTBs) to trade such as border delays, cumbersome regulations, and so on. The TFA is expected to focus governments' attention on the various aspects of trade facilitation, including some that go beyond the written mandate of the TFA. Some of those aspects are technical issues of border management, such as reducing delays, computerizing customs transactions, and streamlining verification and payment procedures. Some others are more genuinely economic, such as streamlining NTBs and improving regulatory design through cost-benefit analysis.

At least some of the trade costs that persist in the world trading system can be attributed to non-tariff measures (NTMs), government policies other than ordinary customs duties that have an impact on the price at which exports and imports are traded, the quantities traded, or both. Such costs are particularly worrisome if they have a discriminatory or protectionist effect or if they violate a country's international commitments. However, even NTMs designed to carry out domestic regulatory objectives—for example, to protect human, animal, or plant health, consumer or workplace safety, or the environment—can have substantial effects on international trade that should be considered when such policies are developed.[1]

This volume discusses some of the analytical methods that can be used to accompany this process. Chapter 2 discusses the broad economic rationale for improving the design of NTMs. Chapter 3 illustrates the main forms of quantifying NTMs and their effects, including inventory approaches, price-based approaches, and quantity-based approaches. It also proposes a new analytical and measurable concept of *regulatory distance* to help in guiding deep integration efforts at the regional level. Chapter 4 discusses the effects of NTMs on household expenditures, poverty, and firm competitiveness. Chapter 5 illustrates how analysis of NTMs can be used to inform policy advice. Chapter 6 concludes.

The work presented here builds on a great deal of previous work on the economics and policy implications of NTMs. For surveys of the broad landscape of NTMs and the policy issues surrounding them, see WTO (2012) and UNCTAD (2013). Treatments of quantitative issues surrounding NTMs that parallel most closely those in this present volume may be found in Deardorff and Stern (1997) and Ferrantino (2006). Useful approaches to policy reform in NTMs can be found in Cadot and Malouche (2012) and Cadot, Malouche, and Sáez (2012).

Note

1. Some of the literature on this topic distinguishes between non-tariff policies that discriminate or create an issue for international obligations and other non-tariff measures, referring to the former as *non-tariff barriers*. Since we are concerned primarily with economic effects, we use the terms *NTM* and *NTB* more or less interchangeably, except where explicitly noted.

References

Arvis, Jean-François, Yann Duval, Ben Shepherd, and Chorthip Utoktham. 2013. "Trade Costs in the Developing World: 1995–2010." Policy Research Working Paper 6309, World Bank, Washington, DC.

Cadot, Oliver, and Mariem Malouche, eds. 2012. *Non-Tariff Measures: A Fresh Look at Trade Policy's New Frontier*. Washington, DC: World Bank.

Cadot, Olivier, Mariem Malouche, and Sebastián Sáez. 2012. *Streamlining Non-Tariff Measures: A Toolkit for Policymakers*. Washington, DC: World Bank.

Deardorff, Alan V., and Robert M. Stern. 1997. "Measurement of Non-Tariff Barriers." Economics Department Working Paper 179, OECD Publishing, Paris.

Ferrantino, Michael. 2006. "Quantifying the Trade and Economic Effects of Non-Tariff Measures." Trade Policy Working Paper 28, OECD Publishing, Paris.

Novy, Dennis. 2013. "Gravity Redux: Measuring International Trade Costs with Panel Data." *Economic Inquiry* 51 (1): 101–21.

UNCTAD (United Nations Conference on Trade and Development). 2013. "Non-Tariff Measures to Trade: Economic and Policy Issues for Developing Countries." United Nations, Geneva.

WTO (World Trade Organization). 2012. *World Trade Report 2012: Trade and Public Policies—A Closer Look at Non-Tariff Measures in the 21st Century*. Geneva: WTO.

CHAPTER 2

The Policy Case for Tackling Non-Tariff Measures

Trade as an Engine of Growth

Whether and to what extent reducing trade barriers provides a boost to growth has been the subject of a long controversy. The main challenge has always been to identify the effect of trade openness in itself on growth as opposed to the effects of a host of other country characteristics, including physical characteristics, macroeconomic policy, governance, and institutions, likely to affect growth.

The first strand of trade-and-growth studies relied on cross-sections of countries, with all of the weaknesses that come with such an approach. In a seminal contribution, Sachs and Warner (1995) devised a binary index of openness to trade (open = 1, closed = 0) aggregating information on tariff and non-tariff barriers (NTBs), exchange rate distortions, the existence of export monopolies (prevalent in the 1980s, particularly in Africa), and a general socialist versus a market-economy label. Growth regressions showed that open economies grew and converged more robustly than closed ones. Although a host of other studies pointed in the same direction (see Edwards [1998] for a review), a critical study by Rodriguez and Rodrik (2001) showed that the genuinely trade-related components of Sachs and Warner's index (tariff and non-tariff barriers) contributed none of the cross-country variation in growth performance; the variation was explained entirely by exchange rate distortions and the presence of export monopolies (or, equivalently, by Africa and Latin America dummies). Their deconstruction exercise suggested that the message delivered by cross-country econometrics was merely that Africa and Latin America had grown slower than other regions—hardly a scoop.

Following the accumulation of data and a general trend in empirical studies, the second strand of trade-and-growth studies relied on panel data techniques, with data organized around "events" (see the vertical lines in figure 2.1), which consist of piling up several years of cross-country data and controlling for country heterogeneity via country markers called *fixed effects*. Carefully identifying the dates of trade liberalization in each country, Wacziarg and Welch (2008) showed

Figure 2.1 Sample Means of Growth and Investment around the Date of Trade Liberalization

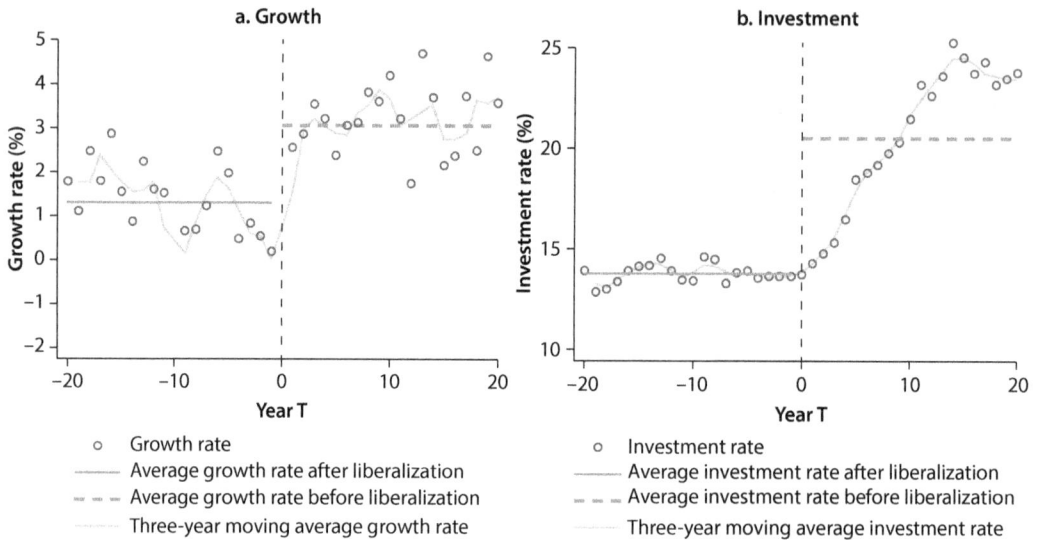

Source: Wacziarg and Welch 2008.
Note: Year T = year of liberalization.

that the evolution of growth rates before versus after liberalization upheld the findings of Sachs and Warner (1995): liberalizing countries experienced modest accelerated growth—on the order of 2 percent per year—after liberalization. Moreover, the growth acceleration was accompanied by a surge in investment, suggesting that the acceleration was fueled not only by total factor productivity (more efficient use of productive inputs) but also by faster accumulation.

Although a significant advance over cross-sectional studies, the exercise of Wacziarg and Welch (2008) was still vulnerable to confounding influences, as episodes of trade liberalization typically coincided with broader reform packages, making it difficult to disentangle the effect of trade liberalization per se from that of other, simultaneous, policy reforms (exchange rate changes, customs reforms, privatizations, and the like).

A third strand of studies resorted to instrumental variable techniques in order to filter out omitted variable and reverse causality biases. In a widely cited study, Frankel and Romer (1999) showed that when the geographic determinants of trade typically used in gravity equations were used as instrumental variables to trade (geography being the one exogenous factor in the whole growth-trade nexus), trade was correlated with income levels, that is, with accumulated growth. The results of Frankel and Romer were later shown not to be robust to the inclusion of latitude and institution-quality variables in the second-stage equation—the equation "explaining" growth by trade.

The basic identification problem that Frankel and Romer's (1999) approach left unsolved was that instruments given by geography were static and therefore confoundable with many other country characteristics. Feyrer (2009b) proposed an original solution to that problem: using the fact that transport costs have declined more rapidly for air transport than for sea transport over the past half-century, he reasoned that country pairs with long sea routes would be more affected by the cost reduction than those with long circle (air) routes. Thus, Feyrer's instrument was the interaction of technology that varied over time but was common to all countries with geographic position that was time invariant but that varied across countries, yielding an instrument that would vary both over time and across countries. On the basis of this identification strategy, he estimated that 17 percent of the variation of income growth across countries between 1960 and 1995 was attributable to technology-induced (exogenous) trade expansion, with an elasticity of income growth to trade growth of about 0.7. In a follow-up study (Feyrer 2009a), he used the surprise closure of the Suez Canal after the 1967 Six-Day War as a natural experiment, allowing him to filter out all confounding influences other than trade in goods—the relevant magnitude if one thinks of policy implications in terms of trade infrastructure. In accordance with intuition, countries for which the closing of the canal increased sea-route distance the most recorded (a) the strongest drop in sea-route distance when the canal closed and (b) the greatest recovery when it reopened in 1975, with a somewhat lower trade elasticity of income (between 0.15 and 0.25).

Most recently, Estevadeordal and Taylor (2013) applied a treatment-effects approach to tariff reductions on capital equipment after the Uruguay Round, instrumenting them with historical events that would make countries more or less willing to liberalize. Again, the hypothesis that trade liberalization had a small but positive growth effect was upheld.

Thus, after years of controversy, the presumed link between trade liberalization and growth has withstood the econometric pounding. The effect is small, but it does exist. This finding has largely vindicated, although ex post, the drive to reduce the high tariff and non-tariff barriers that many low-income countries were imposing until the 1980s. Beyond its obvious policy implications, the trade-causes-growth finding also implies that any type of trade barrier, whether policy induced or not, is bound to hamper growth. These and other findings have prompted a wider exploration of the factors that hinder trade, in particular for low- and middle-income countries, which we discuss in the next section.

High Trade Costs in Spite of Liberalization

Traditional barriers to international trade have been substantially reduced around the world. Tariffs have been lowered progressively over the past 30 years as part of structural adjustment programs, a multilateral round of trade talks, and many regional negotiations, leading to lower tariffs across the board (figure 2.2).

Likewise, quantitative restrictions and command-and-control measures (price controls, prohibitions) have largely been phased out, with a few exceptions. As an illustration, in the Middle East and North Africa region in 2001 and 2011, technical regulations gradually replaced command-and-control measures (figure 2.3).

Figure 2.2 Average Tariffs, by Country Income Level, 1980s–2000s

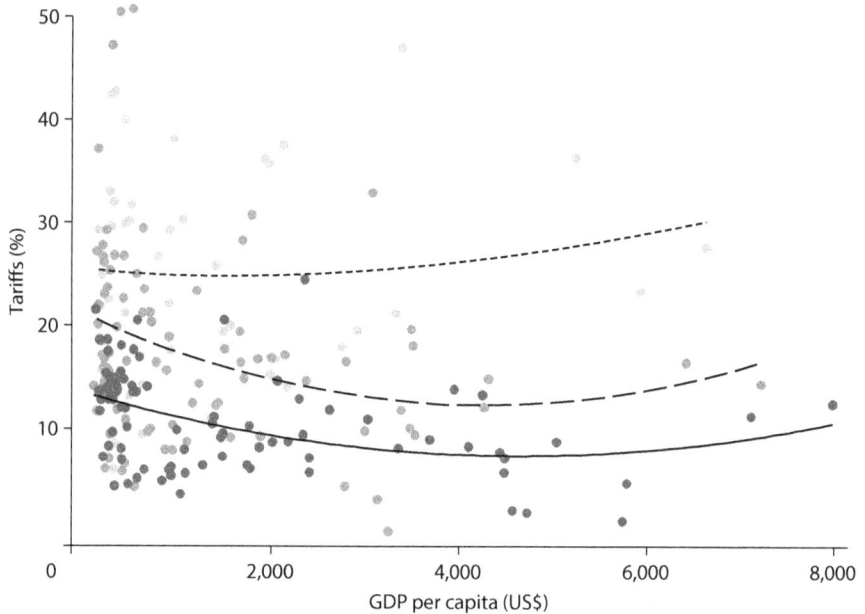

Source: World Bank using the United Nations Conference on Trade and Development's Trade Analysis Information System.
Note: Dots represent average tariffs at the country level as follows: green dots for the 1980s, orange dots for the 1990s, and blue dots for the 2000s. Similarly, the upper quadratic fit curve (short dashes) is for the 1980s, the middle curve (long dashes) is for the 1990s, and the lower curve (solid) is for the 2000s. GDP = gross domestic product.

Yet overall trade costs have remained high, in particular for low-income countries. One way to understand overall trade costs is to put the gravity equation on its head and to estimate trade costs indirectly from the ratio of actual trade to estimated internal trade, as suggested by Arvis and others (2013) and Novy (2013). Plotting the resulting curves shows that the extent of the decrease in trade costs has been moderate, in particular for low-income countries (figure 2.4).

Several factors tend to raise the cost of international transactions relative to domestic ones, including physical, cultural, and linguistic distance. Notwithstanding these factors, non-tariff measures (NTMs) are potentially powerful contributors. There are several reasons for this. First, NTMs have proliferated recently as consumers in industrial countries have become increasingly concerned about food safety and other consumer hazards. As a result, the regulation factory never sleeps. For instance, every year the United States adopts between 3,000 and 4,000 new federal regulations (Dudley 2013). In low- and middle-income countries, the concentration of rule-making and verification functions in the same agencies (say, national standards bureaus) creates a conflict of interest, as standards bureaus issue unnecessary regulations just to generate or maintain a lucrative business of inspection fees. Second, these regulations are increasingly complex because they trail technology. As manufactured products are made of a large number of components, each of

Figure 2.3 Transformation of Non-Tariff Barriers in the Middle East and North Africa Region, 2001 and 2011

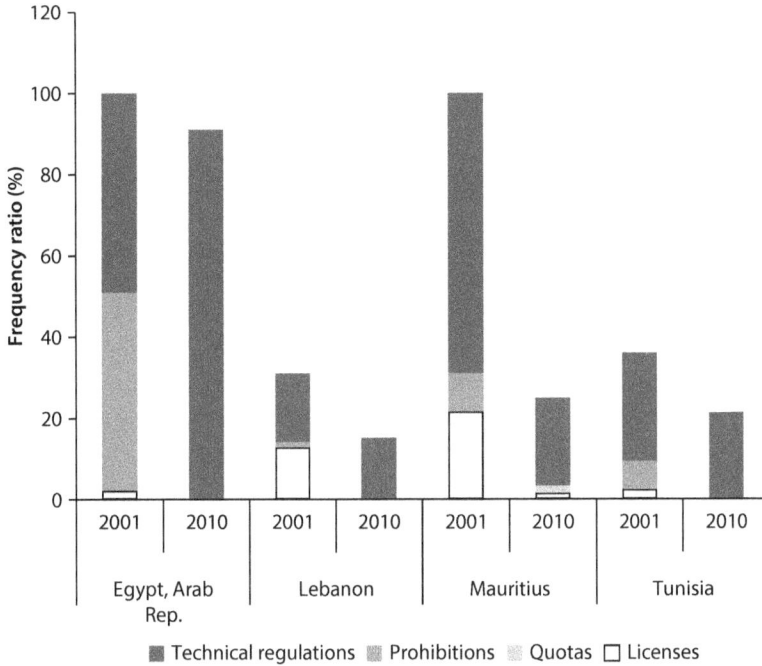

Source: World Bank and United Nations Conference on Trade and Development non-tariff measures data.
Note: The frequency ratio of non-tariff measures is the proportion of Harmonized System six-digit (HS6) products covered by at least one non-tariff measure.

Figure 2.4 Evolution of Gravity-Simulated Trade Costs, by Country Income Level, 1996–2009

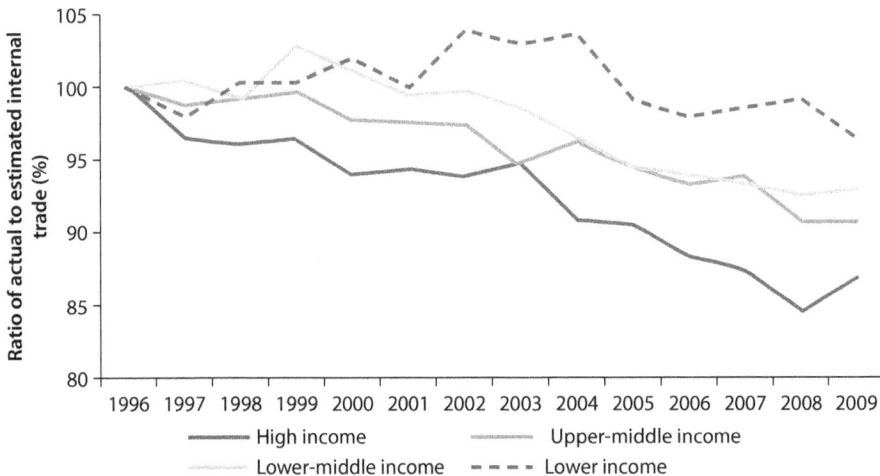

Source: World Bank and United Nations Economic and Social Commission for Asia and the Pacific (ESCAP) statistical data.

Reforming Non-Tariff Measures • http://dx.doi.org/10.1596/978-1-4648-1138-8

which is subject to separate regulations, mastering compliance for a final consumer product and all of its components requires a mass of information. Last, and relatedly, information on regulations is not always easily available, particularly in low- and middle-income countries. This is partly a result of the sheer number of regulations and partly a result of the lack of client orientation in many regulatory agencies.

Streamline, Not Eliminate: The Basic Welfare Economics of NTMs

Countries have a wide range of motivations for regulating imports using means other than tariffs. Some NTMs, such as quantitative restrictions or nonautomatic licensing requirements, have, in most cases, the motive simply to limit imports per se. In other cases, governments may have legitimate reasons to regulate in order to protect the safety and health of humans, animals, or plants or the natural environment. To the extent that such social regulation involves the regulation of goods, it must be imposed on imports as well as domestically produced goods. Such regulation generates benefits, as well as the costs of inefficiency associated with protection. Ideally, these benefits will outweigh the costs associated with restricting imports, so that the existence of the NTM improves welfare. As we shall see, there are even cases in which the volume of imports may actually increase as the result of imposing an NTM. Thus, a "guillotine" approach, which simply targets large numbers of NTMs for elimination without inquiring what purpose they are meant to serve, may not be the best way to go about reform (Cadot, Malouche, and Sáez 2012, chapter 3).

The simplest case of an NTM is a quantitative restriction or quota. Insofar as it is designed merely to restrict imports, the use of quotas generates the same type of costs associated with protection administered through tariffs.[1] In principle, a quota can be designed that is equivalent to any given tariff—one simply works out the quantity of imports that would be expected under a particular tariff, based on conditions of supply and demand, and sets the quota at that level.

However, all of the effects of a quota are not the same as a tariff. In the ideal case of perfect competition, the market equilibrium arising from a quota is identical to the equivalent tariff. Even under perfect competition, however, there are distributional consequences. The revenues from a tariff go to the importing country's government, while the rents from having the right to import go to quota holders. The quota holders may be residents of the importing country or the exporting country, depending on the arrangement. If quotas are allocated based on historical production or imports, quota holders may engage in "rent seeking"—overproducing the good, or producing the good at lower quality, to qualify for more quotas (Feenstra 2004; Krueger 1974).

In the absence of perfect competition, quotas and tariffs generally are not equivalent in welfare terms. In the case of monopoly power in the domestic market, a monopolist may continue to exercise market power under a quota, which would not be available under a tariff; a monopolist may not charge more than the tariff-inclusive price for imports but can maximize profits subject to the residual post-quota demand curve (Bhagwati 1965). Accordingly, quotas can lead to lower welfare than tariffs.

Moreover, when products are differentiated by quality, the presence of a quota, or voluntary export restraint (VER), can distort the mix of products offered by importers. Because the number of imported units is fixed, it is in the interest of the importer to offer higher-priced, higher-quality units to earn a higher markup. The most well-known case of this kind is the VER imposed by Japan on exports of automobiles into the United States from 1981–94, originally in response to the threat that the United States would impose a quota on imports. Japanese automakers shifted their offerings for the U.S. market away from compact cars and toward more high-end vehicles as a result (Feenstra 1988).

The more complex case arises when governments impose measures to deal with market failures. These may include issues with product safety; human, animal, or plant health; or environmental protection; particularly in cases where consumers are lacking full information about the side effects of producing or consuming particular goods (WTO 2012). If the issue involved can apply both to domestic and imported goods, a system of regulation to address the issue will invariably involve NTMs.

If a regulation is well-founded, the benefits arising from the regulation should exceed the visible costs imposed on producers and consumers. Whether this is the case may be determined by an appropriate regulatory impact assessment, although imperfect information often makes such assessments challenging. In the case of internationally traded goods, such an assessment should take into account the possibility that the regulation could distort the choice between domestic and imported goods in some way unrelated to the regulatory objective. This is embodied in the language of the World Trade Organization's (WTO) Agreement on Technical Barriers to Trade (https://www.wto.org/english/docs_e/legal_e/17 -tbt_e.htm, downloaded June 4, 2018 [Article 2.2]) to the effect that "technical regulations shall not be more trade-restrictive than necessary to fulfil a legitimate objective, taking account of the risks non-fulfilment would create."

The question of whether the changes to trade patterns caused by NTMs are justified by regulatory benefits may be seen differently by the exporter and importer, potentially leading to trade disputes. A case in point is mandatory country-of-origin labeling (mCOOL) implemented by the United States in 2005 for fish and shellfish and for meat in 2009.[2] These regulations were challenged by Canada and Mexico at the WTO, resulting finally in the decision by the U.S. Congress to abolish the regulation in 2015.[3] The supporters of mCOOL argued that such labeling was necessary for U.S. consumers to be able to assess the health and safety of meat, fish, and shellfish. The opponents argued that the costs of tracing the imported products were so high that it was easier for U.S. buyers of meat to simply refuse to buy imports; they further argued that U.S. consumers were not obtaining that much information from the labels and perhaps were not even reading the labels.

A system of product regulation on imports, for example, an inspection regime, may have the effect of reassuring consumers of the quality of imported goods, and increasing demand for such goods. At the same time, the costs of implementing the regulation will tend to push prices up, thereby reducing demand for imports. In principle, this means that quality regulation on imported goods could actually increase the volume of imports if the effects of the regulation in increasing demand outweigh the effects of the cost of implementing the regulation. However, if the costs of implementing the regulation are large enough to outweigh the increased in demand for imports caused by better information about product quality, then imports will decline.[4] A regulation falling on imports that is optimal for the regulating country from the cost-benefit standpoint may cause imports either to fall or rise. This effect is independent of the question of whether the regulation is optimal or well-designed. An NTM that fails even to achieve its basic regulatory objective and is costly to implement may be a good candidate for streamlining or elimination, even apart from considerations of how streamlining or elimination may affect international trade. These basic considerations should be kept in mind as readers proceed to chapter 5, where we discuss in more detail how quantitative analysis can be applied to the reform of policies regarding NTMs.

Regional Efforts at Tackling NTMs

As multilateral efforts to reduce NTBs have progressed only slowly, some regional secretariats have tried to impose NTB reduction, harmonization, and mutual recognition agendas in order to reduce regulatory differences and the abuse of regulatory measures for protectionist purposes. For instance, reducing NTBs to trade features prominently in efforts of the Association of Southeast Asian Nations (ASEAN) to promote economic integration in the region, reflecting a widespread view that NTBs have superseded tariffs as relevant barriers to trade. In particular, the ASEAN Economic Community blueprint has mainstreamed the reduction of NTBs in regional integration efforts and improved trade facilitation through the use of single windows.

The ASEAN Trade in Goods Agreement (ATIGA), adopted in 2008, set a schedule for eliminating NTBs in three stages. The approach consisted of classifying them into three categories: green for NTMs that were not NTBs (that is, justified measures), amber for NTMs whose trade restrictiveness could be discussed, and red for NTMs that were clearly NTBs. ASEAN member countries were supposed to submit lists of NTMs, which the ASEAN would then classify into green, amber, or red. The classification would be reviewed by member countries, after which measures would be examined and prioritized for elimination by negotiating bodies, including the Coordinating Committee on the Implementation of the Common Effective Preferential Tariff (CEPT) for the ASEAN Free Trade Area.[5]

The ATIGA mechanism suffers from an incentive problem: it expects governments to provide information that will then be put on the bargaining table, although they have an incentive to hoard it instead. It also expects governments to set up interministerial coordinating mechanisms to centralize information on regulations issued by various agencies. The problem is that governments are expected to overcome a collective action problem to provide a public good—market access for regional partners.

East Africa has tried a slightly different approach, with the Common Market for Eastern and Southern Africa (COMESA) Secretariat setting up an NTB monitoring mechanism with assistance from donors (see Cadot, Malouche, and Saéz 2012). Unlike the ASEAN mechanism, the COMESA mechanism relies on the private sector to flag issues with NTBs rather than on member countries; in principle, incentives are better. As in ASEAN, NTBs are to be classified by order of urgency. In 2009, the EAC Council adopted the East African Community (EAC) Time-Bound Program for the Elimination of Identified NTBs to identify "quick wins" and build momentum. The program identified 33 NTBs for elimination in 2008, classified into four categories, from A to D, by degree of urgency. The exercise was repeated in 2010, identifying 47 NTBs for elimination.

However, while more NTBs were being identified, reflecting the political realities, they were pushed toward the less urgent categories, as shown in figure 2.5, and the identification of "quick wins" proved difficult in the end. Ultimately, the lack of follow-up on complaints has led to some disaffection with the private sector mechanism.

In addition to their attempt to negotiate the elimination of NTBs at the regional level, countries in the Asia-Pacific region have also adopted a sectoral approach to harmonization and mutual recognition that seems to be delivering results. At the time of writing, the ASEAN Consultative Committee on Standards and Quality was working on implementation of the Hanoi Plan of Action for standards harmonization and mutual recognition arrangements.[6]

Figure 2.5 Number of Non-Tariff Barriers Identified for Elimination in the East African Community Time-Bound Program, by Priority, 2008 and 2010

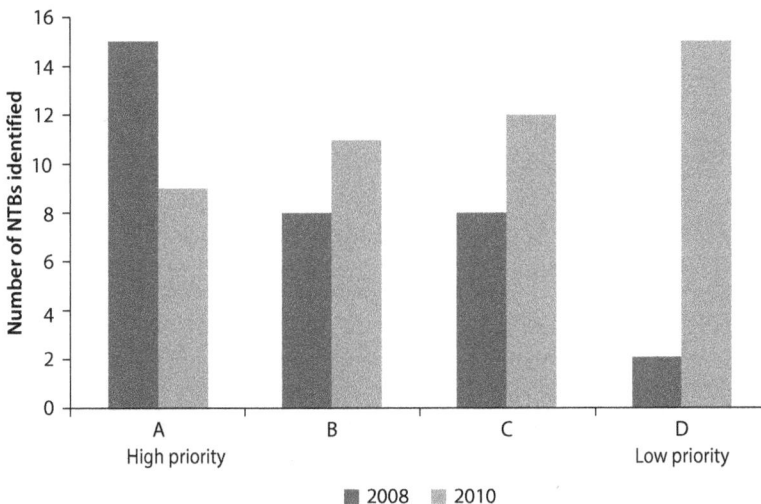

Source: Cadot, Malouche, and Saéz 2012.
Note: EAC = East African Community; NTB = non-tariff barrier.

Reforming Non-Tariff Measures · http://dx.doi.org/10.1596/978-1-4648-1138-8

ASEAN regulators and the industry have been working to harmonize technical requirements and remove technical barriers to trade (TBTs). The ASEAN Secretariat is working on a cosmetic directive intended to guide national regulations in member countries as the basis for mutual recognition—a model close to that in force in the European Union (EU), where the EU Commission sets broad guidelines in regulations and directives and lets member countries adapt their own legislation, ensuring that key provisions are sufficiently close to enable mutual recognition.

A mutual recognition arrangement for electrical and electronic equipment was endorsed by the ASEAN economic ministers. In preparation for its implementation, member countries have undertaken activities to favor the convergence of conformity-assessment procedures. A mutual recognition arrangement for telecommunications equipment was initiated by the ASEAN Telecommunications Regulators' Council and finalized as early as 2000. Finally, a comparative study of ASEAN regulatory regimes for pharmaceuticals has been completed, with several areas identified for harmonization. An ASEAN Common Technical Dossier has been developed for the registration of pharmaceutical products, which is to serve as a basis for application of the mutual recognition arrangement.

Part of the difficulty encountered by regional NTB elimination programs is that what one country considers to be an unnecessary NTB, another may consider to be a legitimate NTM, as societal preferences, regulatory legacies, administration practices, and levels of development may differ even within a regional trading bloc. In chapter 3, we propose a measure of "regulatory distance" that will subsume in a quantitative way how far apart regulatory systems are and that could measure progress in fostering regulatory convergence, possibly for use in a regional integration scorecard.

In sum, whereas some progress is being achieved in key sectors for the regional economy, the experiences of both ASEAN and East Africa highlight how difficult it is to eliminate NTBs when they are approached from a trading-concessions angle. In the next section, we propose an alternative approach in which each country views NTM streamlining as part of a broader but largely domestic regulatory improvement agenda.

Making NTM Streamlining Part of Country-Level Competitiveness Agendas

NTBs restrict market access, but they do not necessarily improve the profitability of domestic producers. The reason is that poorly designed regulations create inefficiencies that are difficult to track down, with sometimes unexpected losers, as illustrated by the case of Indonesia's steel standard. For instance, poorly designed or administered technical or sanitary standards can hurt importers of intermediate products. If those importers are also exporters—as is often the case—poor NTM design will hurt national competitiveness as much as market access.

Viewing the elimination of NTBs through the lens of mutual concessions is not just a conceptually misguided approach; it may even be counterproductive if it induces governments to postpone reform in order to keep bargaining chips for eventual negotiations.

Here we suggest distinguishing clearly between NTMs and NTBs and pursuing two distinct objectives: (a) eliminating NTBs and (b) improving regulations for other NTMs with the aim of minimizing their costs for the private sector. Given an objective of improvement rather than elimination, the problems involved in making NTMs less trade distorting are essentially problems of better regulation, which are similar to those encountered in the improvement of domestic regulations.

Mexico's experience with regulatory reform, summarized in box 2.1, illustrates some of the difficulties involved in broad-ranging regulatory improvement programs.

Box 2.1 Mexico's Experience with Regulatory Reform

The drive for regulatory reform in Mexico came in early 1995, when the so-called "Tequila crisis" of December 1994 highlighted the need to modernize the economy. As tariffs could not be raised to protect jobs because of the country's regional engagements under the North American Free Trade Agreement, it became clear that the government's only option was to reduce the costs that heavy regulations impose on domestic producers.

Mexico embarked on a top-down program of regulatory reform driven by a small group of high-level technocrats with strong support from the presidency. The process was institutionalized through the creation of a regulatory improvement agency, the Economic Deregulation Unit (UDE). The UDE was placed under the Secretariat of Trade's authority but given, by presidential decree, broader authority than the Secretariat of Trade itself. Some critics believe that the decision to place the UDE under a ministry's umbrella rather than making it a strictly independent agency was at the root of its subsequent weakening. In the early days, the UDE gained credibility and clout by initially targeting "low-hanging fruits"—regulatory reforms that were widely seen as urgent; in actuality, it embarked on an ambitious agenda of deregulation rather than tackling a laundry list of small-scale, low-visibility regulations and NTMs. The UDE required all ministries not just to notify it of their regulations, but also to provide justification for them. This shamed ministries into eliminating the silliest formalities, leading to the elimination of 45 percent of regulations by 1999 (IFC 2008).

A second step in institutionalization of the regulatory reform process was to create the Economic Deregulation Council, a consultative body bringing together representatives of regulation-issuing ministries, the UDE, business, labor unions, and academia (IFC 2008). Although without formal sanction powers, the council, which met quarterly, reinforced the UDE's strategy of exposing silly, harmful, or special-interest-driven regulations. Distortionary regulations often make their way through the political process because of an imbalance between concentrated beneficiaries (lobbies) and dispersed societal interests. Around the

box continues next page

Box 2.1 Mexico's Experience with Regulatory Reform *(continued)*

council's table, lobby-driven ministries, which the president required to be represented by the ministers themselves (not by low-level substitutes), found themselves surrounded by representatives of wider interests; that requirement alone made it more difficult to ram through harmful measures. The UDE would review ministries strategically, starting with friendly ones (Trade and Foreign Affairs) and turning to more difficult ones (Interior, Communications, Transportation) later on (Salas 2009).

The third and final step was to pass the Federal Administrative Procedures Act and transform the UDE into a formal federal agency, Comisión Federal de Mejora Regulatoría (COFEMER), in 2000. The law's objective was to ensure that new regulations would obey standards of transparency and rationality by assessing the regulatory process of specialized agencies. Already since 1996, federal agencies were required to submit regulatory impact assessments for new regulations (Salas 2009). To reinforce its powers, COFEMER was given a staff of 60 professionals, a budget of US$5 million, and independent status with a president-appointed head (although it was still within the Secretariat of Trade). For instance, it could undertake its own cost-benefit analyses and had the brainpower to do so. However, key limits to its power, such as the exclusion of all tax-related matters, were maintained because of opposition from the Finance Ministry.

International support was key. Many of the ideas in which the technocrats had been trained were "in the air" abroad, as regulatory reform and state retrenchment agendas were pushed forward in the last quarter of the twentieth century in New Zealand, the United Kingdom, the United States, and elsewhere (in particular, the Organisation for Economic Co-operation and Development regulatory reform agenda). The UDE got support in many ways, including technical assistance from peer agencies in Canada, the United Kingdom, and the United States, and this support was important to overcome isolation.

However, in spite of its institutionalization, the regulatory reform process was only as strong as the president's political backing. When elections returned a hostile parliamentary majority, partisan politics significantly slowed down the reform process. By that time, reform fatigue in the face of weak growth (although Mexico's disappointing performance was due to a variety of factors that had little to do with COFEMER's performance) had eroded political support for further regulatory reform. In 2003, COFEMER lost a key battle against the telecommunications sector, waiving its right to issue an opinion on the sector's draft regulation (which incumbent operators favored). The same year, the head of COFEMER was abruptly replaced, and the agency was without a head for several months.

Source: Haddou 2012; interviews with key participants.

Mexico's experience suggests that four key ingredients need to be present to make regulatory reform viable:

1. A consistent and mutually reinforcing reform agenda and a strong and permanent *political anchor,* such as a binding trade agreement
2. *International support* in the form of technical assistance to the regulatory improvement body and international (typically regional) cooperation in regulatory improvement

3. A credible *institutional setup* revolving around a strong oversight body with independence, competence, and high-level political support
4. Engagement of national administrations—in particular, middle-level civil servants—in a regulatory impact assessment process for new regulations and NTMs, taken seriously and used in conjunction with systematic exposure and consultation with stakeholders.

More recently, under the impulse of ASEAN's regional NTM-streamlining agenda, Cambodia has put in place an NTM committee (NTMC), which can be seen as a model. The NTMC's mandate, as defined by the subdecree setting it up, can be subsumed into three broad headings:

1. *Transparency:* (a) collect, update, and disseminate data and information on NTMs, (b) notify (ASEAN and WTO), and (c) prepare an annual report.
2. *Evaluation:* (a) review and evaluate existing NTMs and make recommendations and (b) review draft regulations.
3. *Improvement of procedures:* (a) liaise and ensure coordination, (b) develop implementation guidelines, and (c) provide training.

The NTMC will be endowed with a technical secretariat for the analytical tasks pertaining to evaluation. The secretariat is to be staffed with young economists, with the World Bank providing training. The workflow of NTM reviews is shown in figure 2.6. The secretariat can take complaints about NTMs from the

Figure 2.6 Workflow of Planned NTM Reviews in Cambodia

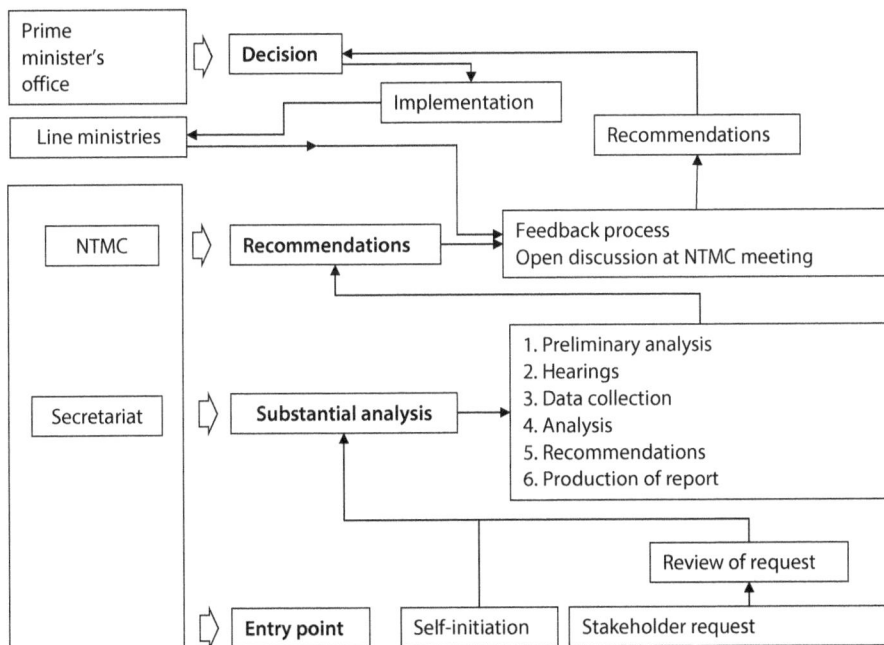

Note: NTM = non-tariff measure; NTMC = NTM committee.

private sector and investigate them; alternatively, the NTMC can initiate its own investigations.

The NTMC and its secretariat are housed in the Ministry of Finance, a strong ministry, which may give it the clout necessary to tackle issues effectively.

Notes

1. Or nonautomatic licensing, voluntary export restraints, or other policies that operate primarily by restricting the quantity of trade directly—though there are separate issues involved with these.
2. See https://www.ams.usda.gov/rules-regulations/cool.
3. See https://www.wto.org/english/tratop_e/dispu_e/cases_e/ds384_e.htm.
4. See WTO (2012), p. 63, for a simple graphical exposition of this point.
5. See https://www.ams.usda.gov/rules-regulations/cool.
6. See https://www.wto.org/english/tratop_e/dispu_e/cases_e/ds384_e.htm.

References

Arvis, Jean-François, Yann Duval, Ben Shepherd, and Chorthip Utoktham. 2013. "Trade Costs in the Developing World: 1995–2010." Policy Research Working Paper 6309, World Bank, Washington, DC.

Bhagwati, Jagdish. 1965. "On the Equivalence of Tariffs and Quotas." In *Trade, Growth, and the Balance of Payments: Essays in Honor of Gottfried Haberler,* edited by Robert E. Baldwin and Gottfried Haberler. Chicago: Rand-McNally.

Cadot, Olivier, Mariem Malouche, and Sebastián Saéz. 2012. *Streamlining Non-Tariff Measures: A Toolkit for Policymakers.* Washington, DC: World Bank.

Dudley, Susan E. 2013. "OMB's Reported Benefits of Regulation: Too Good to Be True?" *Regulation* 36 (2): 26–30.

Edwards, Sebastian. 1998. "Openness, Productivity, and Growth: What Do We Really Know?" *Economic Journal* 108 (447): 383–98.

Estevadeordal, Antoni, and Alan M. Taylor. 2013. "Is the Washington Consensus Dead? Growth, Openness, and the Great Liberalization, 1970s–2000s." *Review of Economics and Statistics* 95 (5): 1669–90.

Feenstra, Robert C. 1988. "Quality Change Under Trade Restraints In Japanese Autos." *Quarterly Journal of Economics* 103 (1): 131–46.

———. 2004. *Advanced International Trade: Theory and Evidence.* Princeton, NJ: Princeton University Press.

Feyrer, James. 2009a. "Distance, Trade, and Income: The 1967 to 1975 Closing of the Suez Canal as a Natural Experiment." NBER Working Paper 15557, National Bureau of Economic Research, Cambridge, MA.

———. 2009b. "Trade and Income: Exploiting Time Series in Geography." NBER Working Paper 14910, National Bureau of Economic Research, Cambridge, MA.

Frankel, Jeffrey, and David Romer. 1999. "Does Trade Cause Growth?" *American Economic Review* 89 (3): 379–99.

Haddou, Ali. 2012. "Streamlining NTMs: How Mexico Did It." In *Non-Tariff Measures: A Fresh Look at Trade Policy's New Frontier*, edited by Olivier Cadot and Mariem Malouche, 247–70. Washington, DC: World Bank.

IFC (International Finance Corporation). 2008. *Regulatory Transformation in Mexico: 1988–2000*. Washington, DC: IFC and World Bank.

Krueger, Anne O. 1974. "The Political Economy of the Rent-Seeking Society." *American Economic Review* 64 (3): 291–303.

Novy, Dennis. 2013. "Gravity Redux: Measuring International Trade Costs with Panel Data." *Economic Inquiry* 51 (1): 101–21.

Rodriguez, Francisco, and Dani Rodrik. 2001. "Trade Policy and Economic Growth: A Skeptic's Guide to the Cross-National Evidence." In *NBER Macroeconomics Annual 2000*, edited by Ben S. Bernanke and Kenneth Rogoff, 261–338. Boston, MA: National Bureau of Economic Research.

Sachs, Jeffrey, and Andrew Warner. 1995. "Economic Reform and the Process of Global Integration." *Brookings Papers on Economic Activity* 26 (1): 1–118.

Salas, Fernando. 2009. "Regulatory Reform, Institution Building: Lessons from Mexico." Public Policy for the Private Sector Note 282, World Bank, Washington, DC.

Wacziarg, Romain, and Karen Horn Welch. 2008. "Trade Liberalization and Growth: New Evidence." *World Bank Economic Review* 22 (2): 187–231.

WTO (World Trade Organization). 2012. *World Trade Report 2012. Trade and Public Policies: A Closer Look at Non-Tariff Measures in the 21st Century*. Geneva: WTO.

CHAPTER 3

The Big Numbers: Do NTMs Matter?

How Prevalent Are NTMs? The Inventory Approach

There are various approaches for identifying the importance of trade measures and assessing their effects on international trade. Methodologies include simple inventory measures, computation of price gaps, and the estimation of ad valorem equivalents (AVEs).

The whole field of research on non-tariff measures (NTMs) faces the challenge of incomplete and problematic data. For example, official data on NTMs, such as those gathered by the United Nations Conference on Trade and Development (UNCTAD) or submitted to the World Trade Organization (WTO), often have significant gaps and do not by themselves indicate the trade restrictiveness or economic impact of the measures addressed. Data from business surveys or complaint-based sources suggest areas of concern, but do not provide a direct indication of economic impact and can be contaminated by inaccurate perceptions of traders. These data sources and the appropriate caveats in using them are discussed in more detail in appendix A.

With respect to the simple inventory approach, we use three indexes: the frequency index, the coverage ratio, and the pervasiveness score. The frequency index simply captures the percentage of products that are subject to one or more NTMs. The coverage ratio captures the percentage of imports that are subject to one or more NTMs. The pervasiveness score captures the average number of NTMs that apply to a product. The frequency index accounts for the presence or absence of an NTM and summarizes the percentage of products i to which one or more NTMs are applied. In more formal terms, the frequency index of NTMs imposed by country j is calculated as follows:

$$F_j = \left[\frac{\sum D_i M_i}{\sum M_i} \right] . 100, \tag{3.1}$$

where D is a dummy variable reflecting the presence of one or more NTMs and M indicates whether there are imports of good i (also a dummy variable). Frequency indexes do not reflect the relative value of the affected products and thus cannot give any indication of the importance of the NTMs for overall imports.

A measure of the importance of NTMs for overall imports is given by the coverage ratio, which is the percentage of trade subject to NTMs for the importing country j. In formal terms, the coverage ratio is given by the following:

$$C_j = \left[\frac{\sum D_i V_i}{\sum V_i} \right] .100. \tag{3.2}$$

where D is defined as before and V is the value of imports in product i. One drawback of the coverage ratio—or any other weighted average—arises from the likely endogeneity of the weights (the fact that imports are dependent on NTMs). This problem is best corrected by using weights fixed at trade levels that would arise in an NTM- (and tariff-) free world. Otherwise, the coverage ratio would be systematically underestimated. While that benchmark is not attainable, it is possible to soften the endogeneity problem (and test for the robustness of the results) by using trade values of past periods.

These frequency and coverage ratios do not take into account whether more than one type of NTM is applied to the same product. In practice, more than one regulatory measure is applied to many products. For example, a product could be subject to a sanitary standard, a technical measure of quality, and some licensing. Arguably, the greater the number of NTMs applied to the same product, the more regulated the commerce of that product is, especially if measures are from different Harmonized System (HS) chapters.[1] To measure the prevalence of NTMs, the score P in equation 3.3 gives the average number of NTMs, N, affecting an imported product, M:

$$P_j = \left[\frac{\sum N_i M_i}{\sum M_i} \right] . \tag{3.3}$$

We start the descriptive analysis by aggregating all of the data collected and examining the incidence of various types of NTMs. Figure 3.1 illustrates the incidence of NTMs for the 40 countries collected so far, with the European Union (EU) treated as one country. It summarizes the data in terms of the frequency index, the coverage ratio, and the prevalence score for each country for all NTMs as a whole.

The use of NTMs varies considerably across regions, but more so across countries. On average, countries apply some form of NTM for slightly less than half of the approximately 5,000 products included in the Harmonized System six-digit (HS6) classification. This figure varies greatly by country.

For example, within Africa, Senegal and Tanzania use NTMs substantially less than the Arab Republic of Egypt, Kenya, or Uganda. In Latin America, Argentina's use of NTMs is double than that of Chile or Paraguay. In Asia, Bangladesh, the Philippines, and the Syrian Arab Republic use NTMs much more than Cambodia or Indonesia. Although this large variance may be due to the use of different methods of primary data collection, different methods of data collection are likely to explain only part of the variance, as large variance is also found for Latin American countries whose data are collected by the same agency: the Asociación Latinoamericana de Integración (ALADI).

Figure 3.1   Frequency Index, Coverage Ratio, and Prevalence Score, by Country

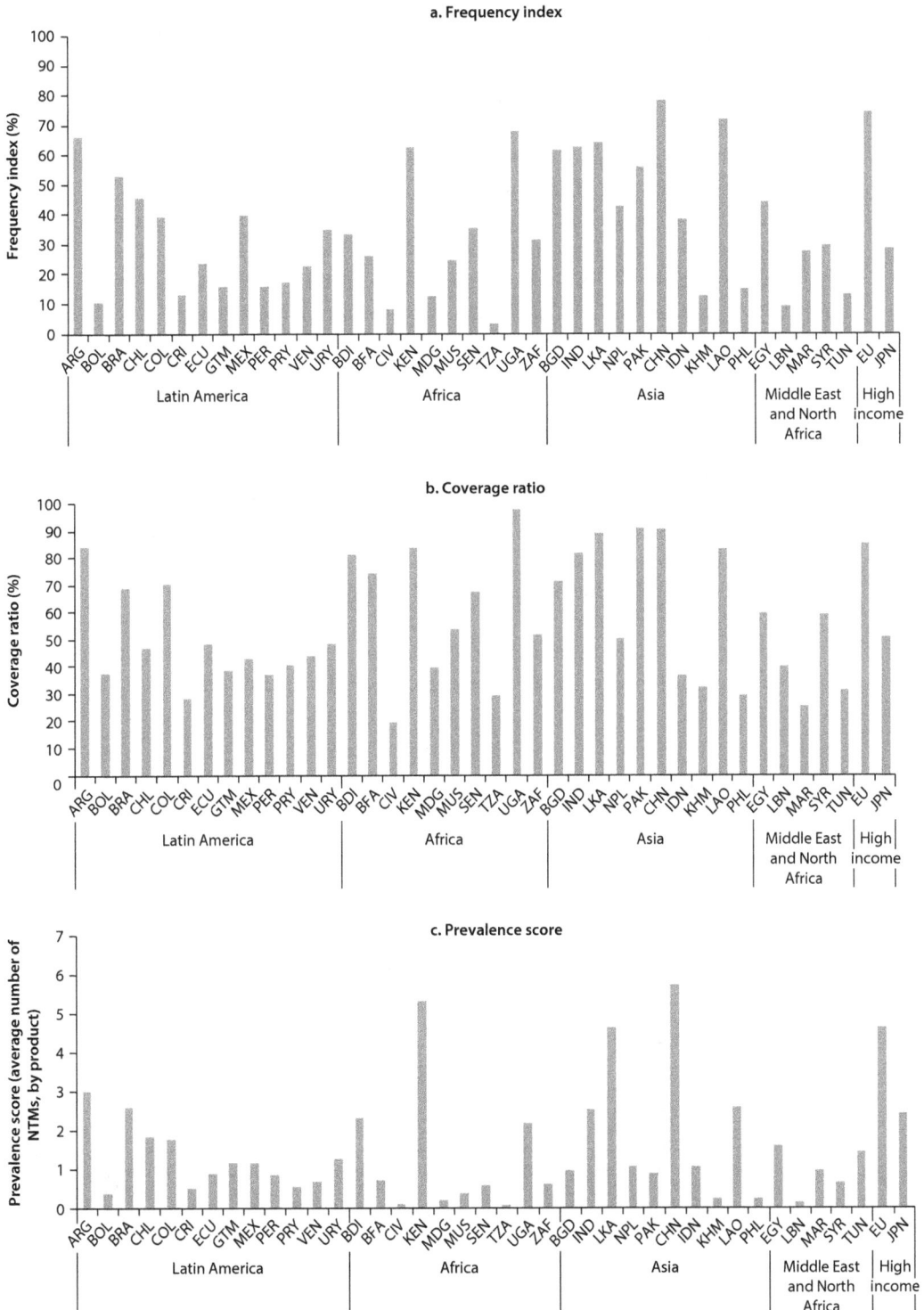

a. Frequency index

b. Coverage ratio

c. Prevalence score

Source: Based on the UNCTAD NTM database.

The incidence of different forms of NTMs varies across geographic areas. Figure 3.2 illustrates the use of NTMs by differentiating the countries in the sample by income: five broad groups of low- and middle-income countries and a high-income group. It shows the distribution of NTMs across three main categories—sanitary and phytosanitary (SPS) measures, technical barriers to trade (TBT), and other NTMs—for the 40 countries. Although SPS measures and TBT are the most used forms of NTMs independent of the region, many countries, especially in Africa and South Asia, still implement a large number of quantitative restrictions (largely in the form of licensing). High-income countries are different from low- and middle-income countries in their use of TBT and average number of NTMs by products. In Africa, countries make heavy use of SPS measures and TBT in an effort to harmonize regulations with their main trading partner, the EU.

We now analyze the impact of NTMs across economic sectors. The use of NTMs varies greatly across economic sectors both for technical and for economic reasons. While some products, such as agricultural products, electrical machinery, and weapons, are highly regulated because of consumer and environmental protection and technical standards, other goods are, by their nature, less subject to laws and regulations. Table 3.1 reports frequency indexes for five broad categories of NTMs for 20 economic sectors.

The use of SPS measures is limited largely to the agriculture sector and products of animal origin, as their control is essential for ensuring the health and well-being of consumers and protecting the environment. As a result, more than 60 percent of food-related products are found to be affected by at least one form

Figure 3.2 Frequency Index, Coverage Ratio, and Pervasiveness Score, by Harmonized System Chapter and Region

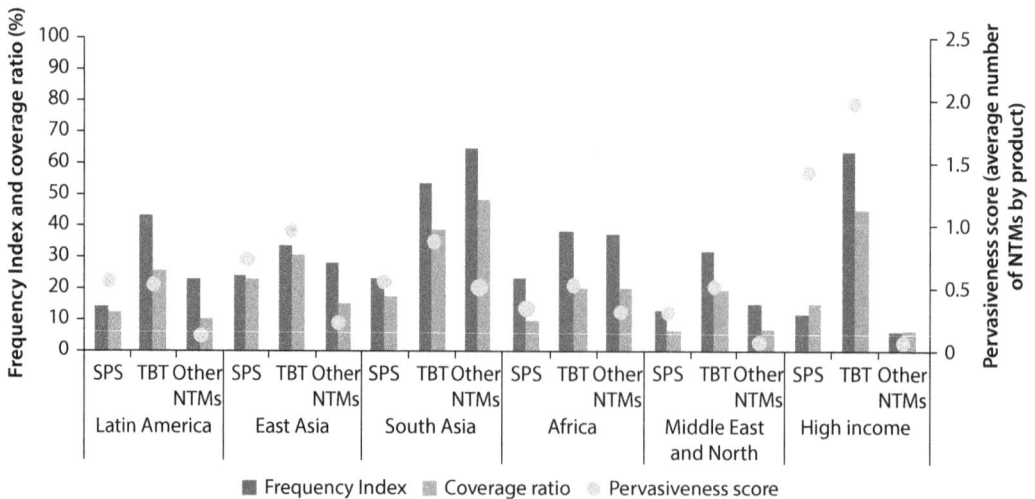

Source: Based on the UNCTAD NTM database.
Note: SPS = sanitary and phytosanitary; TBT = technical barriers to trade; NTMs = non-tariff measures.

Reforming Non-Tariff Measures • http://dx.doi.org/10.1596/978-1-4648-1138-8

Table 3.1 Frequency Index, by Economic Sector

Economic sector	SPS	TBT	Border-control measures	Price controls	Quantity restrictions
Live animals	67.9	29.7	6.1	1.4	6.7
Vegetable products	68.9	31.6	6.5	1.0	5.0
Fats and oil	61.0	51.0	10.4	1.6	5.3
Processed food	65.0	56.9	12.1	1.6	8.6
Minerals products	5.5	27.3	3.4	1.3	2.7
Chemical products	8.8	45.6	5.7	1.5	3.0
Rubber and plastics	4.5	49.8	6.4	1.4	2.7
Rawhide and skins	15.7	18.4	3.7	0.6	12.0
Wood	14.9	16.5	3.9	0.6	0.7
Paper	3.4	27.6	6.0	1.4	3.1
Textile	3.6	47.1	13.4	1.0	14.8
Footwear	2.2	44.4	7.5	1.1	3.0
Stone and cement	4.3	29.3	5.4	1.1	1.5
Base metals	4.2	35.3	11.1	1.5	8.8
Machinery and electrical equipment	5.7	36.5	6.3	1.2	4.8
Motor vehicles	2.4	42.5	6.3	1.7	8.7
Optical and medical instruments	2.2	35.6	9.7	1.2	2.6
Miscellaneous goods	4.1	31.6	5.7	2.1	2.0

Source: Based on the UNCTAD NTM database.
Note: SPS = sanitary and phytosanitary; TBT = technical barriers to trade.

of SPS measure. On the contrary, TBT can suit a much wider set of products, and indeed they are applied more uniformly across economic sectors, with peaks in textiles, footwear, processed food, and chemicals. Border-control measures are distributed widely across economic sectors but concern a more limited number of products. They are more relevant for agricultural products, wooden products, textiles, and footwear. Price control measures such as administrative pricing, antidumping, and countervailing duties are trade-defensive policies that, by their nature, are applied only to very specific products and thus result in low-frequency indexes. Like preshipment requirements, price control measures are more concentrated in agricultural products, textiles, and footwear. Finally, quantity restrictions are applied more or less uniformly across economic sectors, with peaks for agricultural goods, animal products, motor vehicles, and chemical products. In these sectors, particularly sensitive products are often regulated by nonautomatic licenses, quotas, and sometimes outright prohibitions.

We now turn toward the average number of NTMs that a specific country is facing on its partners' markets. This is important for observing how many and how often a country has to comply with external measures. To perform such analysis, we rely on two indexes: the external prevalence index, which captures the average number of non-tariff measures imposed by the trading partners of each country on its export bundle, and the external frequency index, which captures the occurrence of non-tariff measures imposed by the trading partners of each

Table 3.2 External Occurrence of Nontrade Measures for Tunisian Exports

Market	External frequency			External prevalence		
	SPS	TBT	Other	SPS	TBT	Other
World	17.6	79.0	16.9	1.3	3.2	0.2
European Union	8.4	81.8	14.6	0.8	3.1	0.2
France	6.6	87.3	13.8	0.7	3.4	0.2

Source: Based on the NCTAD NTM database.
Note: SPS = sanitary and phytosanitary; TBT = technical barriers to trade.

country on its export bundle. To do so, we weight the number of NTMs and the occurrence of NTMs on the product at the HS6 level by the share of the product in total exports of the reporting country.

At this stage, data collection is incomplete. We have data for 65 countries but not for the United States, so the picture of NTMs that a given country faces on the external market is incomplete.

In table 3.2, we show the external frequency and prevalence indexes for Tunisia, which show how the difference in partners' NTMs and the composition of export bundles to each partner leads to heterogeneity in the indexes across partners. For instance, Tunisia's exports to the world are facing more SPS measures (17.6 percent of exports face at least one SPS measure) than exports to the EU (8.4 percent) and to France (6.6 percent). This is not due to partner specificity, since the EU has the highest frequency index for SPS measures; instead, it is due to the composition of export bundles: Tunisia exports relatively fewer food products to the EU than to the world.

How Stringent Are NTMs? Price-Based and Quantity-Based Methods for Calculating the Ad Valorem Equivalent of NTMs

We now measure the restrictiveness of NTMs. Whether harmonized or not, NTMs generate compliance costs. If, say, electrical wiring must satisfy particular fire-proof requirements, more expensive materials will need to be substituted for cheaper ones. If vegetables must satisfy stringent maximum residual levels of certain pesticides, more expensive ones that leave no trace will have to be used. These costs will be passed on to consumers—although the degree of pass-through depends on many observed and unobserved producer and market characteristics—and ought to be measured.

There are two ways of looking at this effect: through prices and through quantities. When a country imposes a cost-raising NTM on a certain good, the price of that good rises on the domestic market. If the regulatory measures are nondiscriminatory as mandated by WTO rules, the price rise reflects a cost increase that is the same for imported and domestically produced brands of the good. The price rise, in turn, reduces the demand for both imported and domestically produced brands. Thus, there are conceptually three ways of approaching the demand-reducing effect of the measures: by looking at the reduction in the dollar value of trade, at the increase in prices, or at the reduction in the physical quantity of trade. Each approach raises specific data and estimation issues, to which we now turn.

Some Methodological Issues—Handicraft versus Mass-Produced Estimates of NTM Effects

Before looking at specific price- and quantity-based methods for estimating the effects of NTMs, it is desirable to consider some more general issues. In developing estimates of the effects of NTMs, it is necessary to pay attention both to the purpose for which the estimates are going to be used and to the available data. In some cases, it is desirable to look at one or a few NTMs on specific products in specific countries. In other cases, it is desirable to give a broad profile of NTMs on many or all goods for a group of countries or for the world. In the first instance, the analyst is estimating one or a few NTM effects. These estimates can be referred to as *handicraft* estimates of NTM effects. When the analyst is examining hundreds or thousands of country pairs, the estimates can be referred to as *mass-produced*.[2]

Some methods for producing handicraft estimates of NTM effects are discussed in appendix B. These methods involve calculating a price gap or the AVE of an NTM by comparing the distorted price of a product on the market of a country imposing the NTM with the price of a similar product in a similar but undistorted (without-NTM) market. Unfortunately, the conditions for a valid comparison are rarely met in practice; when dealing with a single case, there is no averaging out of confounding influences. The primary challenges are that the prices being compared may be measured at different points in the supply chain and that the quality of goods being compared may be different. Since higher quality is associated with higher prices, so are NTMs. There is a risk that an NTM effect may be identified, when the effect is due to a difference in quality.

Handicraft estimates of NTM effects are most useful when considering individual policies that cover one or a few products. The U.S. International Trade Commission's import restraints studies (for example, USITC 2007) contain product-specific estimates of the effects of quotas on agricultural products, quotas on textiles and apparel (especially in publications prior to the end of the Agreement on Textiles and Clothing in 2005), and other specific barriers. The estimates for Nigeria's import prohibitions reported in this book are also based on handicraft methods.

While handicraft estimates are capable of carefully taking into account the institutional details of the way policies are applied as well as specific features of the data, it is not practical to use them to assess very large numbers of NTMs in multiple countries. These assessments are usually addressed by econometric methods that attempt to control for differences in quality and transport and distribution margins by means of observable variables that proxy for them. The tariff-equivalent approach presented later in this chapter is an example of a mass-produced method. NTM price gaps using mass-produced methods are generally used in the analysis of preferential trade agreements, for example, the analysis of the Trans-Pacific Partnership in Petri and Plummer (2016) and the estimates of NTM effects in U.S.-EU bilateral trade in Berden and others (2009).

While mass-produced estimates are the feasible method for making broad international comparisons or for analyzing trade agreements, the estimated effects are necessarily average effects, either across products or across countries, or both. Thus, they are usually not suitable for policy analysis at the country/product level and cannot serve as a substitute for handicraft methods when product-specific detail is desired. Moreover, they are only as good as the model underlying the estimation, as aptly pointed out by Deardorff and Stern (1998):

> First, by attributing to NTBs [nontrade barriers] all departures of trade from what the included variables can explain, there is a tremendous burden on the model used to explain trade. Indeed, the worse is the model of trade flows, the greater will be the estimates of NTBs, suggesting a considerable upward bias in their estimation. Second, it can be argued that theoretical trade models are capable of determining patterns of trade only when a series of highly unrealistic assumptions are made. In their absence, such models can only determine patterns of trade in an average sense and are not adequate to the task of predicting trade exactly for particular industries and countries. Thus, a departure of actual trade from what is predicted by a regression model may reflect only this indeterminacy and not the presence of NTBs. Third, these approaches can really only make comparisons among industries or countries. They cannot tell us how far trading patterns depart from free trade. For if NTBs restrict trade everywhere, that characteristic may be imbedded in the parameters of the regressions and will not be reflected in the residuals or in coefficients of the dummy variables used to represent unusual circumstances. For these reasons, one should be very cautious in using the results based on estimates of trade models. At best, such estimates may be most helpful for identifying relative levels of non-tariff protection across sectors and countries.

Although Deardorff and Stern's dim view of the value of econometric estimates may be overly pessimistic—after all, gravity-type models predict trade flows accurately and can serve as a reliable basis for the identification of NTM effects—recent attempts have been made to bridge the gap between handicraft and mass-produced methods. If appropriate data are available, nonstochastic methods can be used to estimate hundreds of price gaps one at a time according to a template. While such methods cannot include all information about institutions and quality differences that would be desirable, they represent a viable alternative. One such approach, that of Breaux and others (2014), is discussed in appendix B.

Econometric approaches to the estimation of NTM AVEs can be categorized into three broad types in terms of the dependent variable used on the left-hand side of the equation: dollar trade values, unit values, or quantities. Early work in the area (for example, Kee, Nicita, and Olarreaga 2009) used dollar trade values. However, this approach suffers from a flaw, namely, that when the price elasticity of import demand is unity, trade values do not change whatever the stringency of NTMs (price and quantity effects offset each other), so there is no statistically useable information in the data. Worse, when the elasticity approaches unity, estimated AVEs approach asymptotic values without economic meaning. As one of these asymptotes is infinity, average estimates can be severely distorted, even by a small number of problem cases. For the nontechnical measures ("core" NTBs) studied by Kee, Nicita, and Olarreaga (2009), one could argue that price would not be significantly affected—although recent results suggest that this is not quite true—so the issue was not crucial. For technical measures, however, it can no longer be brushed aside. Accordingly, the recent literature (including Kee and Nicita 2016) has turned to two alternative approaches, one using prices and the other using quantities.

In addition, in their pioneering paper, Kee, Nicita, and Olarreaga (2009) estimated AVEs using import-demand equations, product by product, at the HS6 level (5,000 equations). This meant that identification (a) relied entirely on cross-country variation for a given product and (b) used a small number of observations, as trade flows were aggregated across origins. This approach severely limited the number of parameters that could be estimated. To overcome this problem, more recent papers have used bilateral unit values (price-based methods) or quantities (quantity-based methods). Also, recent work like Cadot, Gourdon, and van Tongeren (2018) or Cadot and Ing (2016) estimates AVEs chapter by chapter using panel-data techniques (where products are like the panel's "individuals" and destinations are the equivalent of its "time" dimension).

Price-Based Methods

Price-based econometric approaches can be thought of as cross-country generalizations of the handicraft price-gap method discussed earlier in this chapter. The major challenge is the unavailability of comparable price data across countries, as domestic price data are not published systematically. National statistical institutes collect detailed price data for the calculation of consumer price indices. However, product classifications vary across countries, and true price data, considered sensitive, are typically not made public; only price indices, normalized by a base year, are made public. Those indices are comparable over time but not across countries; thus, they cannot be used for our purposes, since there is, at the time of publication of this book, only one year of NTM data, and their effect can be inferred only through cross-country comparisons. One exception is the Economist Intelligence Unit's Citydata, which covers consumer prices and salaries in 140 cities from 1990 onward. However, the database is geared to cost-of-living comparisons relevant for expatriates and covers a very particular basket of goods. Moreover, it is not publicly available for researchers and must be purchased from Bureau van Dijk, a commercial agent. The World Bank also calculates comparable consumer prices as part of the International Comparison Program; the data were used to estimate NTM AVEs in Africa by Cadot and Gourdon (2014), but individual prices are not freely available for researchers outside the World Bank.

The only prices observable in absolute form and at a disaggregated level are trade unit values obtained by dividing trade values by quantities. Cadot and Gourdon (2016) used them to estimate AVEs through a simple treatment-effect equation, where NTMs "treat" the prices of some goods in some countries but not others.

There are several problems with using trade unit values to assess the price-raising effect of NTMs. One is that the data are noisy, as customs typically monitor import quantities imperfectly (border taxes are assessed on values, not quantities). However, this may not be too much of a problem for econometric estimation as long as measurement errors are uncorrelated with other regressors on the right-hand side. The second problem is that trade unit values do not include domestic intermediation margins. This is particularly problematic for nontechnical measures, for example, quantitative restrictions with licenses given to domestic distributors; in that case, trade unit values will not reflect the shadow value of the licenses. For technical measures (SPS and TBT), however, compliance costs borne by producers (for example, quality upgrading to satisfy regulatory requirements) are likely to be passed through to trade unit values, although the degree of pass-through may vary depending on market structure (see Asprilla and others 2015).

Notwithstanding these problems, we now provide a brief technical description of the panel price-based approach. Let o, d, and p index, respectively, origin countries, destination countries, and products identified at the HS6 level (at which there are more than 5,000 products). Let do, dd, and dp designate fixed effects (dummy variables) identifying, respectively, origin countries, each destination country, and products. These fixed effects adjust the model's constant for each country and product, neutralizing the influence of all idiosyncratic factors that could affect the level of prices (for the destination country, they control for the cost of living; for the origin country, they control for aggregate productivity). Let UV_{odp} be the unit value of product p imported from country o to country d and $\mathbf{x}_{od}$ be a vector of bilateral determinants of CIF prices, including distance and other factors affecting transport cost. Let A designate type-A measures (SPS) in the Multi-Agency Support Team (MAST) nomenclature, B designate type-B measures (TBT), and "other" lump together all the rest of the measures (quantitative restrictions, prices measures, and the like). Let also

$$I_{dp}^A = \begin{cases} 1 \\ 0 \end{cases} \text{if destination country } d \text{ imposes one or several} \atop \text{type-A NTMs on product } p \text{ or otherwise} \qquad (3.4)$$

For a given HS chapter (estimation being carried out separately, chapter by chapter), the estimation equation is as follows:

$$\ln uv_{odp} = \mathbf{x}_{od}\alpha + \beta_1 I_{dp}^A + \beta_2 I_{dp}^B + \beta_3 I_{dp}^{other} + \sum_p \delta_p + \sum_d \delta_d$$
$$+ \sum_d \beta_{4d}^A \left(\delta_d I_{dp}^A \right) + \sum_d \beta_{4d}^B \left(\delta_d I_{dp}^B \right) + \sum_d \beta_{4d}^{other} \left(\delta_d I_{dp}^{other} \right) \qquad (3.5)$$
$$+ \beta_5 \ln \left(1 + t_{odp} \right) + u_{odp}.$$

The form of this equation makes it possible to retrieve as many estimates of β_{4d} as there are destination countries in the sample, and, thus, to retrieve algebraically different AVEs for a given type of measure applied to a given HS product but by different importing (destination) countries. For example, the approach makes it possible to identify the effect of, say, SPS measures on food-stuffs in each destination country, taking into account unobserved differences in the design and enforcement modalities of regulations. However, because of the data's panel structure, AVEs are chapter (HS2) averages rather than specific product (HS6) estimates.

Because the estimation uses price and not quantity (or dollar-value) variation, the price elasticity of import demand is not involved in the formula to retrieve the AVE. For a given HS chapter and destination country, the average AVE of type-A measures is given by:

$$AVE_{d\hat{p}}^A = e^{\hat{\beta}_4 + \hat{\beta}_{4d}} - 1 \qquad (3.6)$$

where hats designate parameter estimates p refers to an average effect for all HS6 products in the given chapter.

A variant of this approach uses the count of NTMs of a given type (say, A) applied to each product rather than a binary zero-one marker as in equation (3.4). This is possible because the MAST classification is more detailed than the level used in equation (3.5), and the data are collected at the more detailed level. One advantage of this approach is that it takes into account the cumulative burden of NTMs piled up by various bureaucracies on a given product, some-thing that often surfaces in private-sector complaints. Additionally, estimation based on counts (see, for example, Cadot, Gourdon, and van Tongeren 2018, or Cadot and Ing 2016) has proved somewhat more stable than estimation based on binary markers.

A technical point is worth noting at this point. In the quantity-based approach discussed later in this section, when there is no trade in some products between some pairs of countries, the presence of zero trade flows must be taken into account in the choice of the estimator, and the most appropriate choices are maximum-likelihood estimators such as pseudo-poisson maximum likelihood (PPML), zero-inflated negative binomial (ZINB), and zero-inflated Poisson (ZIP). This creates econometric and computing problems in the presence of large numbers of dummy variables (de-meaning, an alternative to the use of dummy variables, is not advisable in two-way panels). However, in the case of price-based estimation, zero trade flows have no well-defined prices and so cannot be taken into account; accordingly, the ordinary least squares (OLS) estimator, which performs well with large numbers of dummy variables, is the sole (and conve-nient) choice. A variant of equation (3.5) interacts NTM variables with a charac-teristic of the destination country (for example, share in world trade) instead of a vector of country dummies, drastically reducing the number of parameters to be estimated. However, this approach, pioneered by Kee, Nicita, and Olarreaga (2009), has led to confusing interpretations. While product-specific estimated AVEs can, seemingly, be mapped one-for-one onto countries (using their share in world trade), they do not describe a particular country's estimated AVE; instead, they simulate what the estimated AVE ought to be at that country's level of trade share. To see the difference between the two approaches, it is useful to think of the following experiment. Suppose that we have two years of data, and between those two years, country d cuts the compliance cost of a given NTM on a given type of products by half through, say, better regulatory design. Estimation using the interaction of NTM variables with country dummies will pick up this reduction. In contrast, estimation using the interaction of NTM variables with trade shares will not pick up any change if the country's trade share does not change.

Table 3.3 and figure 3.3 show average AVEs for 20 HS sections using a price-based approach. In the left-hand side of the table, AVEs are set to 0 for product-country pairs with no NTM; in the right-hand side, such cases are coded as "missing values" and therefore do not enter the average. The former method yields lower average AVEs than the latter. SPS and TBT measures are those with the highest compliance costs. As expected, SPS measures tend to be more constraining for food products, while TBT measures are more obstructive in the equipment and machinery sectors. Other measures such as price control measures (D) or quantity controls (E) are rarely used nowadays, so their impact is smaller.

Table 3.3 Average Ad Valorem Equivalents for Non-Tariff Measures, by Type and Sector

	Average AVE over all HS-6 products				AVE only if NTM is present		
	SPS (A)	TBT (B)	Other NTMs (C, D, or E)	NTM (Total)	SPS (A)	TBT (B)	Other NTMs (C, D, or E)
Animals	16.6	7.9	6.6	31.1	28.0	17.4	15.0
Vegetables	19.0	4.7	3.9	27.6	29.2	9.6	12.6
Fats and oils	10.3	2.0	4.0	16.3	16.4	3.8	10.8
Beverages and tobacco	10.8	9.1	3.4	23.4	18.5	15.1	11.2
Minerals	1.2	6.2	3.1	10.6	22.1	21.8	22.5
Chemicals	2.4	10.8	3.2	16.4	27.1	22.5	13.7
Plastics	0.8	9.9	2.0	12.7	23.7	22.1	13.2
Leather	6.6	5.2	5.1	17.0	44.9	26.3	27.0
Wood products	3.0	4.5	2.7	10.2	29.0	14.3	16.2
Paper	0.7	4.9	3.5	9.1	21.0	19.1	22.9
Textile and clothing	n.a.	9.5	7.9	17.4	n.a.	19.3	14.7
Footwear	n.a.	12.9	4.0	16.9	n.a.	28.3	16.8
Stone and glass	n.a.	10.1	3.5	13.6	n.a.	28.1	20.0
Pearls	n.a.	4.7	3.9	8.6	n.a.	37.6	27.7
Metals	n.a.	8.3	5.3	13.6	n.a.	20.1	13.6
Machinery	n.a.	14.4	6.9	21.3	n.a.	29.9	18.8
Vehicles	n.a.	13.4	6.6	20.0	n.a.	28.7	17.2
Optical and medical instruments	n.a.	15.5	6.1	21.6	n.a.	38.3	19.9
Arms	n.a.	4.2	6.0	10.1	n.a.	35.9	11.2
Miscellaneous	n.a.	11.7	3.1	14.8	n.a.	28.9	19.0
Total	3.6	8.5	4.5	16.6	26.0	23.4	17.2

Note: AVE = ad valorem equivalent; HS = Harmonized Standard; n.a. = not applicable; NTM= non-tariff measure; SPS = sanitary and phytosanitary; TBT = technical barrier to trade.

Figure 3.3 Combined Ad Valorem Equivalents, by Sector

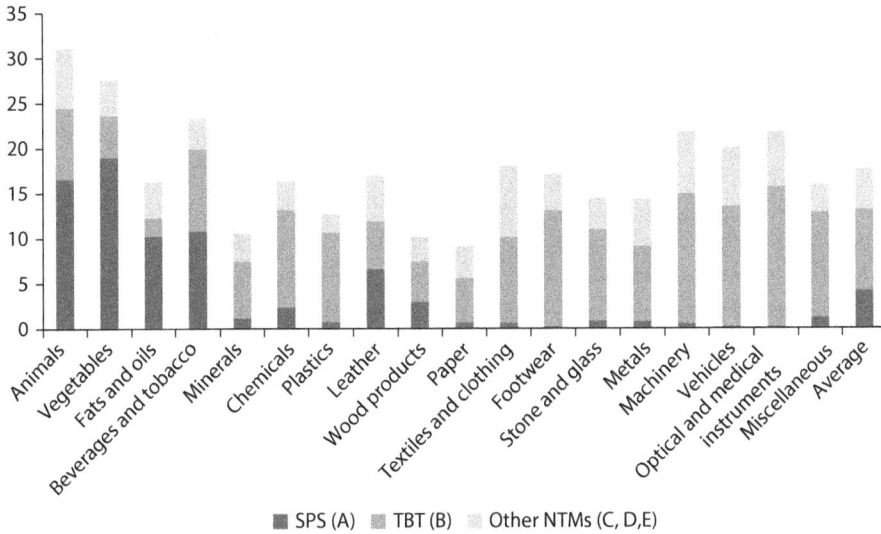

Source: Based on the United Nations Conference on Trade and Development Multilateral Non-Tariff Measure Database.
Note: NTM = non-tariff measure; TBT = technical barriers to trade; SPS = sanitary and phytosanitary.

Quantity-Based Methods

Using the notation we used for the price-based estimation equation and letting q_{odt} be the physical quantity of product p imported by country d from country o, the quantity-based estimation equation is as follows:

$$\ln q_{odt} = f\left[\begin{array}{l} \mathbf{x}_{od}\alpha + \beta_1 I_{dp}^A + \beta_2 I_{dp}^B + \beta_3 I_{dp}^{other} + \sum_p \delta_p \\ + \sum_d \delta_d + \sum_d \beta_{4d}^A \left(\delta_d I_{dp}^A\right) + \sum_d \beta_{4d}^B \left(\delta_d I_{dp}^B\right) \\ + \sum_d \beta_{4d}^{other} \left(\delta_d I_{dp}^{other}\right) + \beta_5 \ln\left(1 + t_{odp}\right) + u_{odp} \end{array} \right] \qquad (3.7)$$

where f is the functional form of the appropriate estimator (not necessarily linear, unlike the OLS used for price-based estimation). After some algebraic transformations involving the price elasticity of import demand, equation (3.7) can be used to retrieve AVEs. However, this is not the main interest of the quantity-based approach and may actually be misleading.

Technical measures (A and B) are generally imposed to address market failures such as information asymmetries or negative externalities,[3] and a strand of theoretical and empirical work suggests that they can work as market-creating catalysts in situations of asymmetric information (see, for example, Henson and Jaffee 2008; Maertens and Swinnen 2009; Swinner 2016; Xiong and Beghin 2016). When the quality of suppliers is heterogeneous and unknown to buyers, regulations can overcome the information deficit and convey a signal that all producers conform to a certain standard, encouraging demand. Thus, good regulations can facilitate trade. In such cases, estimates of β_1 and β_{4d} can add up to a positive effect for some countries, which would yield "negative AVEs." Whereas earlier work on NTMs tended to dismiss such cases as pathological and sometimes to force AVEs to be positive through exponentiation or other tricks, they can actually yield valuable information on the market-creating effect of NTMs.

For example, the distribution of counterfeit drugs has a large negative impact on public health. Inspection and testing requirements on imported drugs are NTMs; depending on how heavy the requirements are, they can have high AVEs on all drugs, including legal ones. Similarly, two-wheelers with two-stroke engines generate toxic smokes with adverse health effects in urban areas. Restrictions on the importation of such products are NTMs; they can be considered, de facto, as trade restrictions when the products are not produced locally.

Combining Price-Based and Quantity-Based Methods

The discussion in the previous two sections suggests that price-based methods and quantity-based methods, far from being substitutes in the search for accurate AVEs, yield different types of information. The following sums up the discussion:

- In the case of nontechnical measures, the effect on trade unit values is indeterminate a priori; it can be positive or negative. By contrast, the effect on quantities is expected to be negative, as those measures are typically commercial ones intended to limit import volumes.
- In the case of technical measures, the effect on trade unit values is unambiguously positive, as compliance costs cannot be negative; by contrast, the effect on quantities is indeterminate, depending on the relative strength of compliance-cost versus market-creating effect.

The case of technical measures recently developed in Cadot, Gourdon, and van Tongeren (2018) is illustrated in figure 3.4, where the vertical axis measures CIF (cost, insurance, and freight) import prices and the horizontal one measures

Figure 3.4 NTM Compliance Costs versus Market-Creating Effects

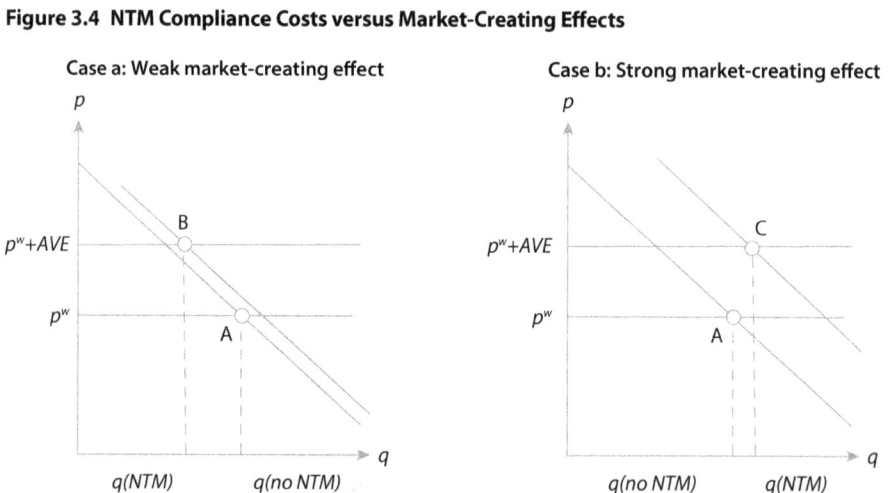

Case a: Weak market-creating effect

Case b: Strong market-creating effect

Source: Calculations based on the United Nations Conference on Trade and Development Multilateral Non-Tariff Measure Database.
Note: Kruskal stress value = 0.208.

physical quantities. In both panels, p^w is the world price in the absence of the importing country's NTM. The difference between the two horizontal lines is the NTM's AVE under full pass-through. The difference between the two demand curves reflects the NTM's market-creating effects discussed previously.

In figure 3.4, case (a), market-creating are weak, so the market equilibrium shifts from A to B and import quantities go down; in case (b), they are strong, so the market equilibrium shifts from A to C and import quantities rise in spite of the NTM's demand-inhibiting effect. Thus, variation in prices can be used to retrieve AVEs, while variation in volumes can be used to assess, qualitatively, the strength of market-creating effects relative to compliance costs. In other words, we are interested in the magnitude of the effect in equation (3.5) but only at its sign in equation (3.7).

When the AVE is positive and import volumes go up, we can conclude that the NTM's market-creating effects outweigh its business costs; the converse is the case when import volumes go down. When the AVE is zero (or statistically insignificant) and import volumes do not change, we can conclude that the NTM is ineffective. Finally, when the AVE is positive and import volumes do not change, the correct interpretation of the NTM's effect is not that it is ineffective, but that its compliance costs are just offset by its market-creating effects. Thus, the approach combining price-based methods with quantity-based ones can disentangle a number of configurations that previous approaches could not.

Figure 3.5 is the empirical counterpart of figure 3.4, showing a scatterplot of log-changes in prices (on the vertical axis) against log-changes in volumes (horizontal axis), aggregated over all HS sections, by importer. Each point is an importer-HS section pair; its vertical intercept is the AVE obtained from price-based estimation (aggregated from HS chapter to section), whereas its horizontal

Figure 3.5 Estimated Equilibrium Changes, by Country

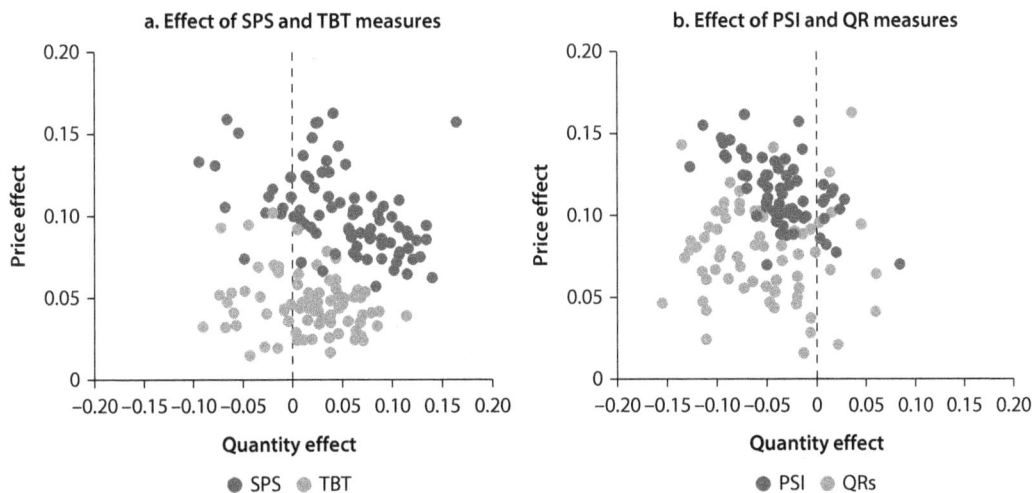

Source: Calculations based on the United Nations Conference on Trade and Development Multilateral Nontariff Measure Database.
Note: PSI: pre-shipment Inspection; QR: quantitative restrictions; SPS = sanitary and phytosanitary; TBT = technical barriers to trade.

intercept is its effect on import volumes obtained from quantity-based estimation (also aggregated from chapter to section).

As expected, our AVE estimates have sharply different interpretations for technical versus nontechnical measures. AVEs estimated from trade unit values for SPS and TBT measures can be safely assumed to reflect compliance costs accurately. SPS and TBT measures have, on average, positive and substantial effects on the trade unit value products, suggesting substantial AVEs; for many countries, however, they also have positive effects on import volumes, suggesting market-creating effects. Pre-shipment inspection (PSI) and quantitative restrictions (QR), in contrast, also have positive effects on trade unit values, suggesting some rent-sharing between importers and exporters, but mainly negative effects on import volumes, as presumably intended.

How Do NTMs Differ? A Regulatory Distance Approach

Measuring Regulatory Differences

A given NTM may be less inhibiting on bilateral trade between countries that have similar or harmonized NTMs than on trade between countries that have different NTMs. For example, if a country imposes certain requirements for food containers and the exporting country imposes the same requirements on its domestic producers, the requirement will be less trade-inhibiting. The reason for this is subtle: whereas the price effect is the same (complying with the regulation requires the use of expensive materials and precautions in the manufacturing) and the demand-reducing effect in the importing country is the same, the similarity of the regulations may divert trade away from other partners that have different types of regulations, which would make countries trade more bilaterally. Thus, at the bilateral level, equation 3.8 could be amended to take into account our measure of regulatory distance—either the product-specific measure introduced in the section on price-based methods, $|n_{olp} - n_{dlp}|$ or the overall country-pair distance:

$$\ln m_{odp} = \delta_o + \delta_d + \delta_p + \beta_1 n_{dp}^{NTM} + \beta_2 \ln(1 + t_{odp}) + \beta_3 D_{od} + x_{od}\gamma + u_{odp} \quad (3.8)$$

where $D_{od} = \sum_l \sum_p |n_{olp} - n_{dlp}|$ is the regulatory distance between countries o and d. The expected sign of β_3 is then negative.

In this section, we propose a *regulatory distance* approach that compares patterns of NTM use across products between one country and another. This approach is of particular value in assessing whether regional convergence exists in the pattern of NTMs or whether NTMs of a given country approach global best practice.[4]

Specifically, we use the structure of NTM inventories (coded in binary form, by 1 if a certain type of measure is imposed on a certain product and 0 otherwise, regardless of the measure's exact wording and stringency) and assess whether two countries apply the same type of measure to the same product by measure-product pair.

Suppose that country A imposes one type of NTM, say UNCTAD classification B840 (inspection requirements), on a given product defined at HS6, say HS 840731 (spark ignition reciprocating piston engines of a kind used for the propulsion of vehicles of HS chapter 87, with a cylinder capacity not greater than 50 cubic centimeters). If country B imposes the same type of measure (coded as B840) on that same product, for the given measure-product pair, countries A and B are said to be similar. We then code the regulatory distance variable as 0. By contrast, if country B imposes a different regulatory requirement, but not B840, or if it imposes no NTM at all on that product, then countries A and B are said to be dissimilar for measure-product pair (B840, HS 840731), and the regulatory distance variable is coded as 1. Formally, let i index countries, k index HS6 products, and j index NTM types, and let I_{ilk} be an indicator function defined by the following:

$$I_{ilk} = \begin{cases} 1 \\ 0 \end{cases} \text{ if country } i \text{ applies NTM } l \text{ to product } k \text{ otherwise} \qquad (3.9)$$

The regulatory distance measure at the measure-product level is the absolute value of the difference between this indicator function between the two countries: $r_{lk} = \left| I_{ilk} - I_{jlk} \right|$.

In the second step, regulatory distances at the measure-product-pair level are aggregated into an overall measure of dissimilarity or regulatory distance at the country-pair level. That is, let N be the total number of observed product-NTM combinations. The country-level regulatory distance measure for countries i and j, D_{ij}, is as follows:

$$D_{ij} = \frac{1}{N} \Sigma_K \Sigma_l \, r_{ilk}. \qquad (3.10)$$

As D_{ij} is normalized by the grand total of product-NTM combinations, it lies between 0 and 1. In our sample, it ranges between 0.009 for trade between Madagascar and Tanzania and 0.304 for trade between China and Nepal.

The analysis above produces large matrixes of regulatory distance measures. These can be conveniently summarized using appropriate graphical methods. The idea is to project bilateral distances onto a plane akin to a map. Mathematical details of the method are given in appendix A. Clearly, the mapping cannot be perfect; with 33 countries to place on the map (we treat the EU as one country, as the regulatory distance among member countries is 0) and arbitrary distances between them, only a 32-dimensional space could provide a perfect representation. As the number of dimensions shrinks, the distortion in the representation of distance grows. If there is no distortion, all points would lie on the 45° line, indicating that the distortion is moderate.

We show the resulting projection on a two-dimensional space in figure 3.6, which shows the results for the overall NTM data. In order to interpret the figure, the axes are arbitrary: they are scaled to fit the range of bilateral distance and merely represent the cardinal points in which distances are mapped. First, a small number of countries stand out for unusual patterns of NTM imposition. Those include China, Morocco, Namibia, Nepal, and Sri Lanka.[5] Second, a core of countries has similar patterns of NTM imposition at the product level, providing a sort of common pattern on which national administrations can draw to

Figure 3.6 Bilateral Regulatory Distance for Manufactured Products and TBT Measures

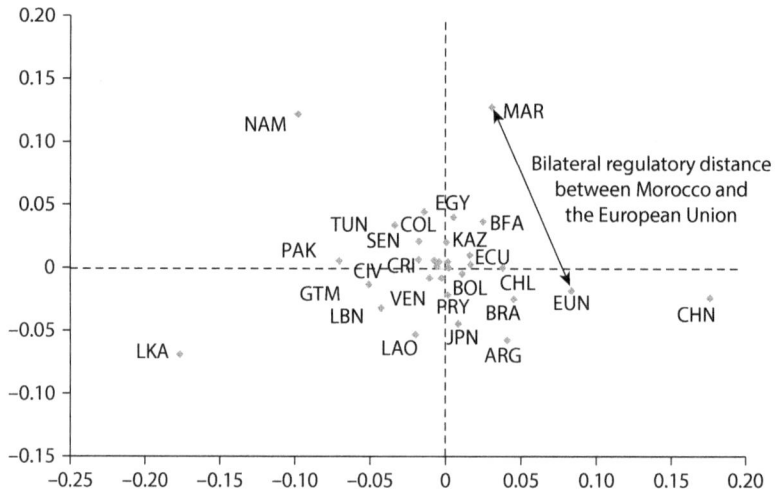

Source: Calculations based on the United Nations Conference on Trade and Development Multilateral Non-Tariff Measure Database.
Note: Chapters over HS99 only; Kruskal stress value = 0.119; TBT = technical barrier to trade.

decide which type of measure to apply to which product, at a fairly detailed level (HS6, with more than 5,000 products; NTM-3, with 64 measures). Morocco's position as an outlier is particularly striking, suggesting that the process of regulatory harmonization envisaged by the Morocco-EU Association Agreement and stated in its Article 51 is still far from completion, even at the relatively crude level of the extensive margin.

Figure 3.5 shows regulatory distance for agri-food products (HS sections 1–4) and SPS measures. There is more dispersion, and the EU now appears as an outlier. As Morocco has harmonized a large number of SPS measures with the EU, the bilateral regulatory distance is now lower (163 percent of the average bilateral distance in the sample, compared with 190 percent in figure 3.7).

For TBT measures, by contrast (figure 3.8), there are both a very strong core of countries with similar patterns of measures and a few outliers, including China, the EU, and, to a lesser extent, Japan.

This representation of regulatory distances can be used in different ways. First, it can be used to assess how effective regional trade agreements are in fostering regulatory convergence. As a first pass, table 3.4 shows the results of a simple ordinary least squares regression of regulatory distance on regional trade agreement (RTA) dummies, using Piermartini and Budetta's (2009) database.

The coefficient in the first column of table 3.4 is negative and significant at the 1 percent level, suggesting that, on average, RTAs reduce regulatory distance between their members. The effect is large: the average RTA cuts regulatory distance by 41 percent (the average bilateral distance in the sample is 0.079). The second column looks at the effect of individual agreements. Only ALADI is

Figure 3.7 Bilateral Regulatory Distance for Agri-Food Products and SPS Measures

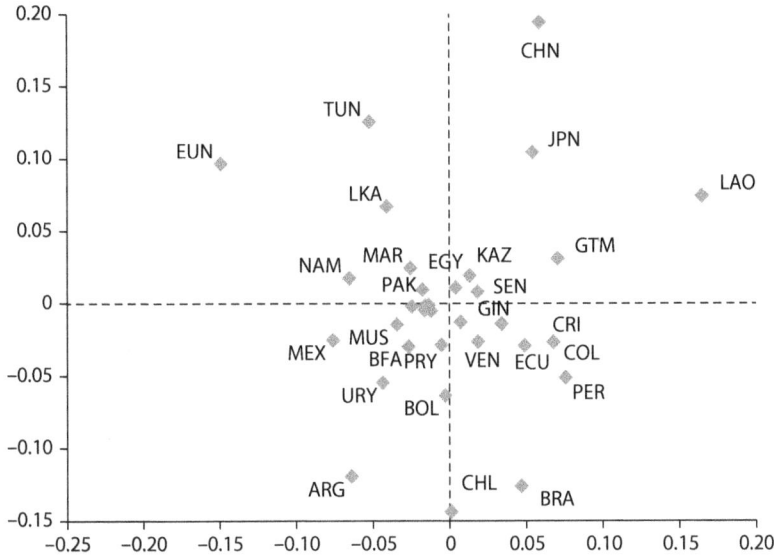

Source: Calculations based on the United Nations Conference on Trade and Development Multilateral Non-Tariff Measure Database.
Note: International best practices (IBP): European Union, Japan; middle-income IBP: Chile, Mauritius, Mexico. Distance is an abstract measure. See the text for details.

Figure 3.8 Bilateral Regulatory Distance for Manufactured Products and TBT Measures

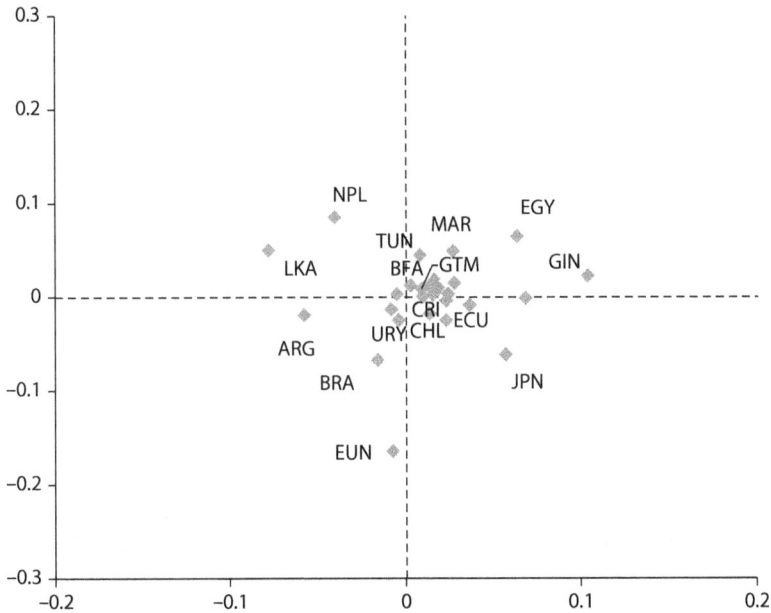

Source: Calculations based on the United Nations Conference on Trade and Development Multilateral Nontariff Measure Database.
Note: Chapters over HS99 only; Kruskal stress value = 0.119; TBT = technical barrier to trade.

Table 3.4 Regression Results for Regulatory Distance and Regional Trade Agreements

	(1)	(2)
Both in the same regional trade agreement (any)	−0.033 (8.07)***	
Both in ALADI		−0.029 (2.83)***
Both in Andean Community		−0.023 (0.77)
Both in CACM		−0.049 (0.72)
Both in COMESA		−0.033 (0.85)
Both in SADC		−0.045 (1.14)
Both in SAFTA		0.018 (0.46)
Constant	0.086 (24.33)***	0.083 (26.15)***
Observations	992	992
R^2	0.01	0.01

Note: Estimator = ordinary least squares; dependent variable = bilateral regulatory distance. Robust *t*-statistics in parentheses. ALADI = Latin American Integration Association; CACM = Central American Common Market; COMESA = Common Market for Eastern and Southern Africa; SADC = South African Development Community; SAFTA = South Asia Free Trade Agreement.
*** $p < 0.01$, ** $p < 0.05$, * $p < 01$.

significant, as other agreements have too few observations in the data set to identify significant effects. Further research is needed to assess if those results carry on in a larger sample and with proper control variables; but the prima facie evidence is encouraging. From a policy perspective, it suggests that RTAs do induce a convergence of regulatory systems at the extensive margin; that is, member states tend to apply similar measures to similar products, facilitating subsequent harmonization in stringency levels.

A Normative Application

In this section, we take a normative stand and propose a tentative assessment of how rational the observed pattern of SPS measures is by using a particular group of countries as the international best practices (IBP) benchmark. These countries include the EU and Japan for high-income countries. As societal preferences may differ between high-income and middle-income countries in terms of the trade-off between product safety and cost of living, the method also uses a middle-income best practices group made up of Chile, Mauritius, and Mexico. All three countries have made efforts to adopt, at least partially, some good regulatory principles. Thus, the distance between the patterns of NTM application between a particular country outside the IBP group and the best practices group can be taken as a (very preliminary) indication of the need to review the pattern of measures in that country.

The results are shown in figure 3.9. Distance from the IBP group is, for all non-IBP countries except Kenya, larger than distance from the middle-income IBP group, suggesting that patterns of NTM use differ systematically between high-income countries (the EU and Japan) and low- and middle-income ones. This is to be expected and suggests that the method makes sense. By and large, the comparison suggests that Indonesia, the Philippines, and Thailand have patterns of NTM imposition that are not too far from those of the middle-income IBP group, compared with other countries in the non-IBP group. The country with the longest distance is the Philippines, suggesting that some technical assistance could be called for in order to rationalize the country's regulatory regime using international experience.

An additional use of this regulatory distance can be to provide evidence that regulatory convergence—or reducing regulatory heterogeneity—reduces trade costs. In order to ascertain this effect, Cadot, Gourdon, and van Tongeren (2018) estimate the measure of bilateral regulatory proximity (inverse of the regulatory distance as calculated in equation 3.10) between the two trading countries. They show the negative correlation between greater similarity (moving to the right-hand side) and the size of the AVEs for technical barriers SPS and TBT (with a price-based method), adding to the evidence that regulatory differences are a key contributor to trade costs related to NTMs (figure 3.10).

Figure 3.9 Patterns of Non-Tariff Measures: Distance from International Best Practices

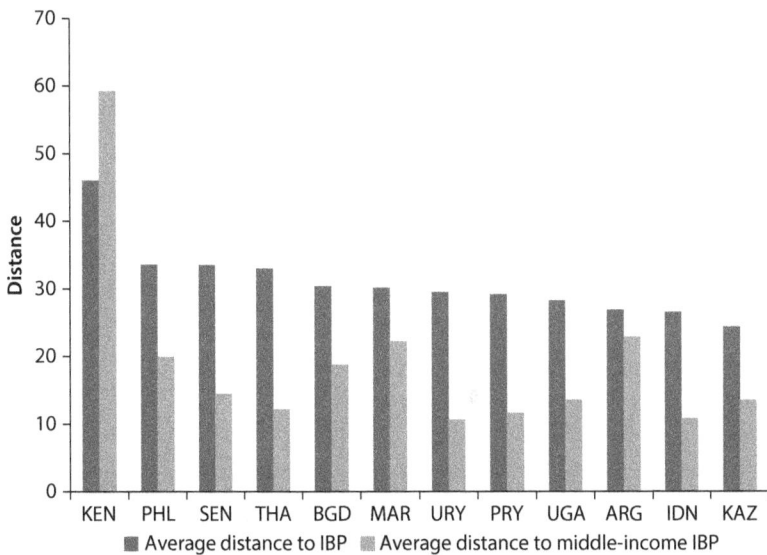

Source: Calculations using the Global No-Tariff Measures Database.
Note: International best practices (IBP): European Union, Japan; middle-income IBP: Chile, Mauritius, Mexico. Distance is an abstract measure. See the text for details.

Figure 3.10 Price Effect versus Regulatory Distance with Partners, by Country

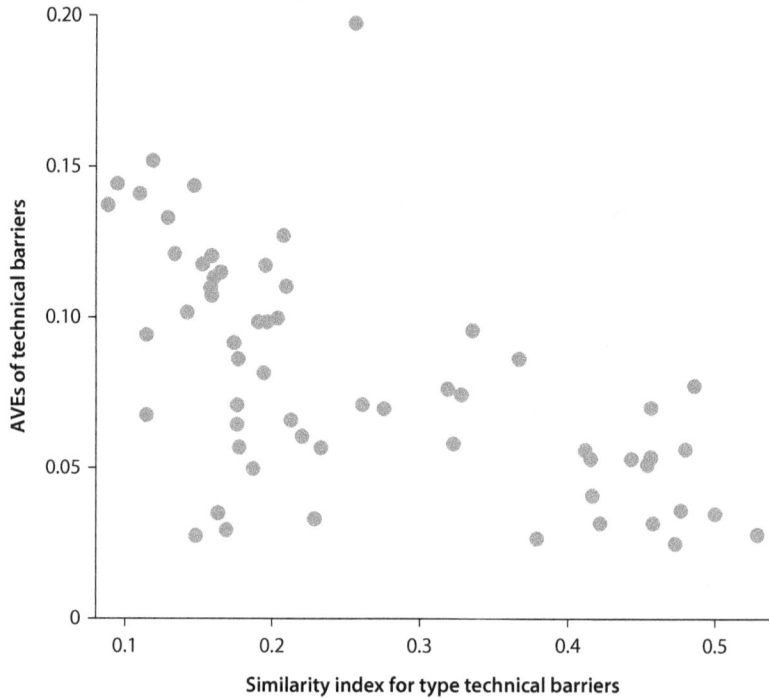

Source: Cadot, Gourdon, and van Tongeren 2018.
Note: AVE = ad valorem equivalent.

Notes

1. The rationale is that measures within the same chapter are similar in nature and thus often impose relatively less burden than measures from different chapters.

2. The distinction between *handicraft* and *mass-produced* estimates is taken from Ferrantino (2006).

3. For example, the distribution of counterfeit drugs has a large negative impact on public health. Inspection and testing requirements on imported drugs are NTMs; depending on how heavy the requirements are, they can have high AVEs on all drugs, including legal ones. Similarly, two-wheelers with two-stroke engines generate toxic smokes with adverse health effects in urban areas. Restrictions on the importation of such products are NTMs; they can be considered, de facto, as trade restrictions when the products are not produced locally.

4. See Chen and Mattoo (2008) for a discussion of the normative issues involved in regional standard making.

5. We recoded Chinese data to transform all NTMs erroneously coded as B for products other than agri-food products (HS chapters 01–24) into A, keeping the last three digits the same.

References

Asprilla, Alan, Nicolas Berman, Olivier Cadot, and Mélise Jaud. 2015. "Pricing-to-Market, Trade Policy, and Market Power." Working Paper 04-2015. Economics Section, The Graduate Institute of International and Development Studies, Geneva.

Berden, Koen G., Josep h Francois, Martin Thella, Paul Wymenga, and Saara Tamminen. 2009. "Non-Tariff Measures in EU-US Trade and Investment—An Economic Analysis." ECORYS Final Report OJ 2007/S 180-219473, ECORYS Nederland BV for the European Commission, Directorate-General for Trade, Rotterdam. http://trade.ec .europa.eu/doclib/docs/2009/december/tradoc_145613.pdf.

Breaux, Michele, Yasnanhia Cabral, José Signoret, and Michael J. Ferrantino. 2014. "Quality-Adjusted Estimates of NTM Price Gaps." Office of Economics Working Paper 2014-08B, U.S. International Trade Commission, Washington, DC.

Cadot, Olivier, and Julien Gourdon. 2014. "Assessing the Price-Raising Effect of Non-Tariff Measures in Africa." *Journal of African Economies* 23: 425–63.

———. 2016. "Non-Tariff Measures, Preferential Trade Agreements, and Prices: New Evidence." *Review of World Economics* 152 (2): 227–49.

Cadot, Olivier, and Ing, Lili Yan. 2016). *Asian Economic Papers* 15 (3): 115–34.

Cadot, Olivier, Julien Gourdon, and Frank van Tongeren. 2018. "Estimating Ad-Valorem Equivalents of Non-Tariff Measures: Combining Price-based and Quantity-based approaches." OECD Trade Policy Papers, No. 215, OECD Publishing, Paris.

Chen, Maggie Xiaoyang, and Aaditya Mattoo. 2008. "Regionalism in Standards: Good or Bad for Trade?" *Canadian Journal of Economics* 41 (3): 836–63.

Deardorff, Alan V., and Robert M. Stern. 1998. "Measurement of Non-Tariff Barriers." Economics Department Working Paper 179, OECD Publishing, Paris.

Ferrantino, Michael. 2006. "Quantifying the Trade and Economic Effects of Non-Tariff Measures." Trade Policy Working Paper 28, OECD Publishing, Paris.

Henson, Spencer, and Steven Jaffee. 2008. "Understanding Developing-Country Responses to the Strategic Enhancement of Food Safety Standards." *The World Economy* 31 (4): 548–68.

Kee, Hiau Looi, Alessandro Nicita, and Marcelo Olarreaga. 2009. "Estimating Trade Restrictiveness Indices." *Economic Journal* 119 (January): 172–99.

Kee, Hiau Looi, and Alessandro Nicita. 2016. "Trade Frauds, Trade Elasticities, and Non-Tariff Measures." Unpublished. World Bank and UNCTAD.

Maertens, Miet, and Johan F. M. Swinnen. 2009. "Trade, Standards, and Poverty: Evidence from Senegal." *World Development* 37 (1): 161–78.

Petri, Peter A., and Michael G. Plummer. 2016. "The Economic Effects of the Trans-Pacific Partnership: New Estimates." Working Paper 16-2, Peterson Institute of International Economics, Washington, DC.

Piermartini, Roberta, and Michele Budetta. 2009. "A Mapping of Regional Rules on Technical Barriers to Trade." In *Regional Rules in the Global Trading System*, edited by Antoni Estevadeordal, Kati Suominen, and Robert Teh, 250–315. Cambridge, U.K.: Cambridge University Press.

Swinnen, Johan F. M. 2007. *Global Supply Chains, Standards, and the Poor: How the Globalization of Food Systems Affects Rural Development and Poverty.* Wallingford, UK: CABI.

USITC (U.S. International Trade Commission). 2007. *The Economic Effects of Significant U.S. Import Restraints: Fifth Update 2007*. Publication 3906. Washington, DC: USITC, February.

Xiong, Bo, and John Beghin. 2016. "Disentangling Demand-Raising and Trade-Cost Effects of Maximum Residue Regulations." In *Nontariff Measures and International Trade*, edited by John Beghin, 105–08. Singapore: World Scientific.

CHAPTER 4

Which NTMs Matter for Household Expenditures, Poverty, and Firms' Competitiveness?

This chapter takes up the effects of non-tariff measures (NTMs) on households and firms. The effect on household welfare and poverty is largely mediated by prices. NTMs increase trade costs, but these costs may or may not be transmitted completely to border prices because pass-through is incomplete or, put differently, because they are partially absorbed by trade cost margins. With household survey data and under appropriate assumptions, it is possible to impute changes in NTMs to changes in household welfare and poverty headcounts through the price channel.

Changes in trade costs induced by NTMs can also affect firms, particularly those involved in regional or global changes in value. Firm-level data on inputs and trade exposure could, in principle, be used to measure NTM impacts on firm profitability, entry, and exit. In this chapter, we pursue a less ambitious approach and generate some stylized facts on the kind of NTMs most likely to be relevant for intermediate-goods trade in four archetypal value chains: apparel, footwear, autos, and electronics.

Non-Tariff Measures and Poverty

The extent to which household expenditure is affected by a given NTM depends on the change in domestic prices induced by it. The magnitude of this change, in turn, depends on its sensitivity to changes in border prices due to an imposition (or a change or a removal) of an NTM, which is enforced at the border.[1] This pass-through effect then affects the cost of living across the entire spectrum of households along the income distribution. Changes in border prices affect consumer welfare through two direct channels. The first of these is the consumption channel: as NTMs increase the domestic price of the consumption basket, consumers are worse off because they need more financial resources to afford their initial consumption bundle. The second is the production channel: as some households may be employed in sectors affected by an increase in prices, some families may be better off because their labor wages may increase.[2] This section develops a two-step methodology to explore the implications of NTMs for the cost of living and to approximate the monetary impact for households of observed or simulated policy changes in NTMs.

Increase in the Cost of Living Induced by NTMs

The first step combines ad valorem equivalents (AVEs) and household consumption patterns to describe the degree to which NTMs increase the cost of living across the income distribution.[3] Let i denote a household unit, l denote a product defined according to the household survey (HHS) product nomenclature, which is typically more aggregated than the Harmonized System six-digit (HS6) nomenclature (the trade nomenclature at the level at which AVEs and NTMs are defined), and k denote a product at HS6. Let $\bar{a}_l = \frac{1}{n_l}\Sigma_{k \in l}\,\hat{a}_k$ be the simple average of the estimated AVEs of NTMs imposed on all HS6 products k belonging to HHS category l. A consumption-weighted AVE of NTMs imposed on household i's consumption basket is defined as follows:

$$a^i = \Sigma_l \omega_l^i \overline{a_l}, \tag{4.1}$$

where ω_l^i represents the weight of product l in household i's consumption basket. Since this measure is computed for every household unit i, variations across centiles of the income distribution indicate the degree to which NTMs affect different types of households according to their income level and their consumption shares. Inventory measures can also be aggregated at the household level.[4] Employing this approach, Cadot and Gourdon (2014) find that the incidence of sanitary and phytosanitary (SPS) measures is regressive in Kenya, with consumption-weighted average AVEs ranging between about 9 percent for the 5th centile and 7 percent for the 95th centile (figure 4.1).

Poverty Impact of Observed or Simulated NTM Policy Changes

The second step analyzes ex ante or ex post changes in prices generated by a variation of the trade-related regulatory environment of the country. The empirical approach builds on the methodology of Nicita (2009) and Porto (2006). The extent to which household consumption is affected by prices depends on the expenditure share of each traded commodity and the price variation. The special distribution of price changes across households may not be uniform, as the price pass-through effects are expected to be different between urban and rural areas (Hasan, Mitra, and Ural 2007).[5] A policy shock that changes prices has two first-order effects on households: a change in the poverty line, as the cost of purchasing the poverty bundle changes, and a change in the distribution of income, as the returns to some factors of production adjust.

Figure 4.1 Consumption-Weighted Ad Valorem Equivalent (AVE) for Sanitary and Phytosanitary (SPS) Measures Faced by Kenyan Households

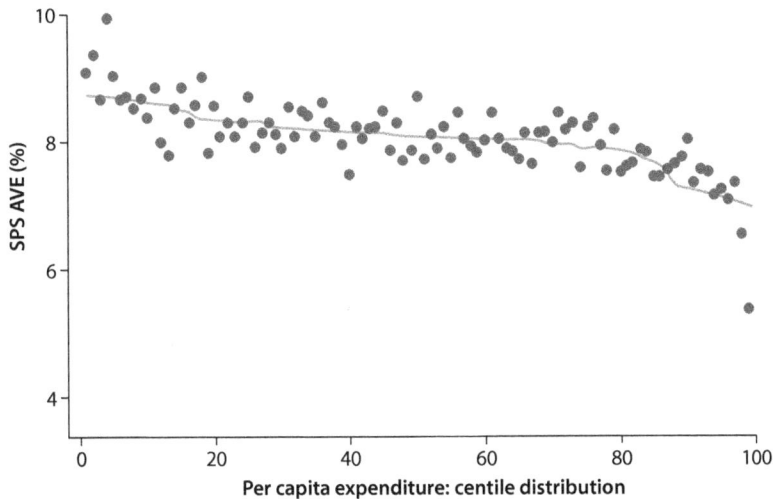

Bandwidth = 0.25.

Source: Cadot and Gourdon 2014.
Note: This figure shows the simple average value of *a* for each centile of the income distribution. Only SPS measures affecting foodstuff products are considered. The line is the smoother regression.

The first effect is estimated by defining the poverty line as $z = \sum_l p_l q_l$, where p_l is the price of good l, and q_l is the quantity determined in constructing the poverty line. Holding the required quantities constant and abstracting from any substitution effects between consumption products within household units, the change in the (log) rural or urban poverty line induced by a change in the price of good l is given by the following:

$$\hat{\Delta} \ln z_r = \sum_l \hat{\alpha}_{rl} \hat{\beta}_r \Delta \ln p_l(\text{NTM}) \quad \forall r = \{rural, urban\}, \quad (4.2)$$

where α_{rl} is the weight attached to good l in region r and $\beta_r \Delta \ln p_l(\text{NTM})$ is the price effect that is transmitted from the NTM policy shock to the household in region r. For an ex post analysis, changes in prices are measured by variations in border prices. For an ex ante analysis, changes in prices are proxied by variations in AVEs.[6] The weights $\hat{\alpha}_{rl}$ are estimated using the average budget share spent on food products by r households in the second quintile of the distribution. The pass-through elasticity $\hat{\beta}_r$ is estimated by regressing domestic r prices for commodities l on corresponding information on international prices, exchange rates, tariffs, and non-tariffs (box 4.1).

The second effect estimates the shift in the distribution of income, which is assumed to happen only through wages. Porto (2006) demonstrates that the proportional change in the total income of household i is given by the

Box 4.1 NTM Pass-Through to Domestic Prices

An important part of investigating the relationship between NTMs and the cost of household consumption is to examine how changes in border prices are transmitted to the consumer. Many empirical models assume a perfect pass-through, where any changes in border prices (due to changes in non-tariff measures) are fully and instantaneously transmitted to retail prices and, therefore, to consumers. However, differences in market structure and the degree of domestic market connectivity to international borders affect this transmission mechanism. These factors are unlikely to be distributed evenly across regions. Consequently, the effect of NTMs on domestic prices will likely be diverse within the country.

Building on Feenstra (1995), Nicita (2009), and Marchand (2012), we construct a measure of the pass-through elasticity that varies across regions using the following framework:

$$\ln P_{rlt} = \beta_0 + \beta_1 \ln P_{lt}^* + \beta_2 \ln(1 + \tau_{lt}) + \beta_3 \ln e_t + \beta_4 \delta_{lt}^{ntm}$$
$$+ \beta_5 rural + \beta_6 rural * \delta_{lt}^{ntm} + \beta_7 \xi_{lt} + \beta_8 \eta_t + \varepsilon_{rlt}, \tag{B4.1.1}$$

where P_{rlt} is the domestic price of good l in region r at time t, P_{lt}^* is the world price, τ_{lt} is the ad valorem tariff, e_t is the exchange rate in domestic currency, δ_{lt}^{ntm} is a dummy variable indicating the presence of an NTM (or the count of a given type of NTMs), $rural$ is a dummy variable equal to 1 if the region is rural, ξ_{lt} represent product-specific trends, η_t are year fixed effects, and ε_{rlt} is the error term. The year fixed effects control for time-varying factors that are common to all regions and products, the product-specific trends control for changes in the costs of production, technology, or inputs across time. The rural dummy takes regional price differences into account.

Because a primary concern is to measure the effect of changes in NTMs on domestic prices for urban and rural households, the empirical specification includes an interaction term between the rural dummy and the presence of an NTM. The parameter β_4 indicates the pass-through elasticity from NTM changes to rural prices, whereas $\beta_4 + \beta_6$ indicates the pass-through elasticity from NTM changes to urban prices. The model can also be modified to investigate whether the extent of pass-through varies for different type of products. The likely pattern of price transmission is expected to be lower in rural areas given that consumers and producers in these places tend to be more isolated from the rest economy.

elasticity of the wage earned by each member in the household with respect to the price (p_l):

$$\widehat{\Delta y^i} = Y^i \left(\sum_m \theta_m^i \hat{\varepsilon}_{\omega_m^i} \right) \hat{\beta}_r \, \Delta \ln P_l (\text{NTM}), \tag{4.3}$$

where $\hat{\varepsilon}_{\omega_m^i}$ is the estimated elasticity of the wage earned by member m in household i with respect to the vector of prices $P()$, and θ_m^i is the share of the labor income of member m in total household i income. Wage-price elasticities are estimated by a Mincer-type equation regressing the wage of individual m on prices of different product categories that m faces, distinguishing between the individual's skill level and the economic sector where m is employed. In its simplest formulation,

$$\ln w_{mr} = \sum_{l=1}^{N} \ln p_r^l(s_m \varepsilon^l) + K\Gamma_m + \mu_{mr}, \qquad (4.4)$$

where S_m is a skilled-unskilled dummy variable and Γ is a vector of workers' characteristics, such as age, age squared, education, gender, marital status, and religion. Applying this methodology, Reyes and Kelleher (2015) explore the poverty impact of streamlining SPS regulations affecting beef, bread and pastries, chicken meat, and dairy products in Guatemala.[7] The authors consider a scenario where AVEs get halved, reflecting a policy aimed at rationalizing the use and operation of SPS measures affecting these products. Results indicate that this policy could reduce urban extreme poverty rates from 5.07 to 4.91 percent. This would mean lifting approximately 20,000 people out of extreme poverty in urban areas of Guatemala.

Firms' Access to Imported Inputs

The presence of non-tariff measures in a supply chain or value chain[8] can often be disruptive. Lead firms that manage multicountry global value chains are very sensitive to costs, time delays, and uncertainty. The accumulation of trade costs of any kind in multiple steps of a supply chain has a cumulative negative effect on competitiveness (Ferrantino 2013; World Economic Forum 2013). Of particular importance is the ability to move intermediate goods from one country to another in a low-cost and rapid fashion. Thus, NTMs on imported inputs are particularly important for value chains.

In an attempt to obtain a broad picture of the type of NTMs most commonly encountered in value chains for manufacturing, we use the United Nations Conference on Trade and Development (UNCTAD) NTM inventory for a selection of 15 economies in conjunction with a list of HS codes associated with intermediate goods specific to four types of final products: apparel, footwear, autos and motorcycles, and electronics.[9] The strategy is to measure both frequency ratios and coverage ratios for the types of NTMs picked up by the inventory. In calculating the frequency ratio, all of the tariff lines of the 15 economies are taken together; in calculating the coverage ratio, global imports for 2013 are used. While the economies in the sample are not fully representative, the results may nonetheless be broadly indicative of the types of NTMs most commonly observed on intermediate goods trade.

Tables 4.1 and 4.2 show that, for our sample of intermediate goods, NTMs apply to between 80 and 86 percent of tariff lines and that at least one NTM applies to around 99 percent of imports of intermediates in the industries selected. The most common types of NTMs are technical barriers to trade (TBT). When reckoned by tariff lines (frequency ratio), price controls are the next most common, followed by SPS measures. But when reckoned by coverage ratios (global imports), SPS measures are more common. The apparel value chain is

Table 4.1 Frequency Ratios, by Non-Tariff Measure Chapter Level
Percentages

Indicator	Apparel	Footwear	Autos	Electronics
% of tariff lines with an NTM	80.9	81.7	85.4	81.5
Chapter A: Sanitary and phytosanitary measures	14.6	14.2	11.3	12.1
Chapter B: Technical barriers to trade	30.7	32.0	42.4	42.7
Chapter C: Preshipment inspection and other formalities	4.8	7.1	3.5	2.5
Chapter D: Quantity controls	6.2	7.1	9.6	6.0
Chapter E: Price controls	24.6	21.3	18.5	18.2

Table 4.2 Coverage Ratio, by Non-Tariff Measure Chapter Level
Percentages

Indicator	Apparel	Footwear	Autos	Electronics
% of imports for which at least one NTM applies	99.0	98.7	99.7	99.9
Chapter A: Sanitary and phytosanitary measures	28.8	19.0	22.1	18.7
Chapter B: Technical Barriers to Trade	53.1	78.9	76.6	80.5
Chapter C: Preshipment inspection and other formalities	2.6	0.1	0.1	0.0
Chapter D: Quantity controls	8.8	0.1	0.4	0.7
Chapter E: Price controls	5.7	0.5	0.5	0.0

distinct from the others in two ways. The incidence of TBT measures for apparel is lower than for the other sectors, especially by coverage ratio. However, intermediate apparel goods, such as yarn and cloth, are often subject to a variety of other NTMs that are less common or rare in the other sectors, including SPS measures, quantity controls, price controls, and preshipment inspection or other formalities. Since TBT requirements are often aimed at legitimate policy objectives, this pattern is broadly suggestive of the use of NTMs for intermediate apparel goods, which is more protectionist than in other sectors. Such a conjecture is consistent with the fact that ordinary import duties also tend to be higher for both intermediate and final apparel than for other kinds of manufactured products.

Table 4.3 attempts to capture the particular types of NTMs that are important for particular value chains, calculating the types of narrow four-digit NTMs observed in each of the value chains as a coverage ratio relative to global trade. Many types of general SPS and TBT measures can occur in any of the manufacturing value chains. These include labeling, marking, testing, and registration requirements. In the auto industry, product quality and performance requirements are particularly important, as are certification requirements for TBT. For footwear parts, prohibitions for TBT reasons appear to be important in at least some cases, as are labeling requirements. These requirements may have to do with the various types of materials (leather, rubber, synthetic, or other) used in making footwear.

Table 4.3 Leading Categories of Reported Non-Tariff Measures, by Coverage Ratio

Category of product and UNCTAD code	Description	Coverage ratio (%)
Intermediate apparel		
B300	Labeling, marking, and packaging requirements	9.3
B820	Testing requirement related to TBT	8.9
B320	Marking requirements	8.6
A140	Special authorization requirement for SPS reasons	8.5
A150	Registration requirement for importers for SPS reasons	8.5
A190	Prohibitions or restrictions of imports for SPS reasons, not elsewhere specified	8.5
Intermediate footwear		
B110	Prohibition for TBT reasons	33.1
B310	Labeling requirements	33.0
A140	Special authorization requirement for SPS reasons	6.2
A150	Registration requirement for importers for SPS reasons	6.2
A190	Prohibitions or restrictions of imports for SPS reasons, not elsewhere specified	6.2
B220	Restricted use of certain substances	6.2
B320	Marking requirements	6.2
Intermediate autos		
B700	Product quality or performance requirements	11.3
B830	Certification requirement related to TBT	10.2
B300	Labeling, marking, and packaging requirements	7.5
B820	Testing requirement related to TBT	7.5
A140	Special authorization requirement for SPS reasons	7.3
A150	Registration requirement for importers for SPS reasons	7.3
A190	Prohibitions or restrictions of imports for SPS reasons, not elsewhere specified	7.3
B320	Marking requirements	7.3
Intermediate electronics		
B840	Inspection requirement related to TBT	7.4
B150	Registration requirement for importers for TBT reasons	7.2
A140	Special authorization requirement for SPS reasons	6.2
A150	Registration requirement for importers for SPS reasons	6.2
A190	Prohibitions or restrictions of imports for SPS reasons, not elsewhere specified	6.2
B110	Prohibition for TBT reasons	6.2
B120	Authorization requirement for TBT reasons	6.2
B300	Labeling, marking, and packaging requirements	6.2
B320	Marking requirements	6.2

Note: UNCTAD = United Nations Conference on Trade and Development; TBT = technical barriers to trade; SPS = sanitary and phytosanitary.

Notes

1. The transmission of changes in border prices to domestic prices also varies across geographic zones within a country for a variety of reasons. Transportation costs of imported goods, for example, would differ across states depending on whether the state has a port, the average distance from ports, and the quality of the transportation infrastructure. Differences in market structures or state-specific taxes and subsidies policies could also play a role.

2. This methodology abstracts from second-order effects, such as the substitution of consumption away from those goods that have become relatively more expensive or the impact on the return to land, farm profits, or household remittances.

3. Mapping NTM data with consumption patterns from household surveys readily provides an overview of the measures that are closely related to the well-being of the poor and that, therefore, should be prioritized in any streamlining exercise. See Reyes and Kelleher (2015).

4. Consumption-weighted NTM numbers and frequency ratios can be constructed, respectively, as $n^i = \sum_l \omega_l^i \bar{n}_l$ and $c^i = \sum_l \omega_l^i \bar{c}_l$, where $\bar{n}_l$ and $\bar{c}_l$ are, respectively, the average number and frequency ratio of NTMs imposed on HS product category l.

5. The transmission of border prices may still vary across regions within rural or urban areas. The methodology can be applied to a finer level as long as detailed price information is available.

6. For example, considering the poverty implications of eliminating a given NTM would entail reducing the price of each product by its estimated AVE.

7. Due to the lack of production data in the Guatemalan household survey data, Reyes and Kelleher (2015) looked only at the change in the poverty line.

8. The term *value chain* generally refers to the activities of a lead firm in coordinating production activities in different countries, whether inside or outside the boundaries of the firm, to add value (Taglioni and Winkler 2016). *Supply chain*, while often used synonymously with *value chain*, most commonly refers to the physical movement of goods necessary for the operation of a value chain.

9. The NTM data are available for the following countries: Afghanistan, China, Costa Rica, the European Union, Kazakhstan, the Lao People's Democratic Republic, Lebanon, Madagascar, Mauritius, Namibia, Nepal, Pakistan, Senegal, Sri Lanka, and Tanzania. The product codes are adapted from Sturgeon and Memedovic (2011), in which they are originally expressed in Standard International Trade Classification Rev. 3. For the purposes of this analysis, apparel and footwear have been disaggregated into separate categories. The assistance of Ronald Jansen and colleagues at the United Nations Statistical Division in mapping these codes to HS2007 is gratefully acknowledged.

References

Cadot, Olivier, and Julien Gourdon. 2014. "Assessing the Price-Raising Effect of Non-Tariff Measures in Africa." *Journal of African Economies* 23 (4): 425–63.

Feenstra, Robert C. 1995. "Estimating the Effects of Trade Policy." In *Handbook of International Economics*, vol. 3, edited by Gene M. Grossman and Kenneth Rogoff, 1553–95. Amsterdam: North-Holland.

Ferrantino, Michael J. 2013. "Using Supply-Chain Analysis to Examine the Costs of Non-Tariff Measures (NTMs) and the Benefits of Trade Facilitation." Staff Working Paper ERSD-2012-02, World Trade Organization, Geneva.

Hasan, Rana, Devashish Mitra, and Bezan P. Ural. 2007. "Trade Liberalization, Labor-Market Institutions, and Poverty Reduction: Evidence from Indian States." In *NCAER India Policy Forum 2006/07*, vol. 3, edited by Suman Bery, Barry Bosworth, and Arvind Panagariya, 71–122. New Delhi and London: National Council of Applied Economic Research; Washington, DC: Brookings Institution.

Marchand, Beyza Ural. 2012. "Tariff Pass-Through and the Distributional Effects of Trade Liberalization." *Journal of Development Economics* 99 (2): 265–81.

Nicita, Alessandro. 2009. "The Price Effect of Tariff Liberalization: Measuring the Impact on Household Welfare." *Journal of Development Economics* 89 (1): 19–27.

Porto, Guido G. 2006. "Using Survey Data to Assess the Distributional Effects of Trade Policy." *Journal of International Economics* 70 (1): 140–80.

Reyes, José-Daniel, and Sinéad Kelleher. 2015. "Poverty Reduction through Regional Integration: Technical Measures to Trade in Central America." *Journal of Economic Integration* 30 (4), 644–79.

Sturgeon, Timothy J., and Olga Memedovic. 2011. "Mapping Global Value Chains: Intermediate Goods Trade and Structural Change in the World Economy." UNIDO Development Policy and Strategic Research Branch Working Paper 05/2010, United Nations Industrial Development Organization, Vienna.

Taglioni, Daria, and Deborah Winkler. 2016. *Making Global Value Chains Work for Development*. Washington, DC: World Bank.

World Economic Forum. 2013. *Enabling Trade: Valuing Growth Opportunities*. Geneva: World Economic Forum.

CHAPTER 5

Getting to Policy Advice

Identifying and Flagging Problem Cases

Chapter 4 argued that econometric estimates should not be used to flag problem cases at the country-product level; yet beyond big numbers, policy makers ultimately are interested in identifying problem cases. We now turn to an approach capable of filling the missing link between big numbers and policy advice on the ground.

We explain three real-world cases where robust economic analysis paired with substantial stakeholders' engagement helped countries to understand the impact of non-tariff measures (NTMs) and to support policy reforms.

Registration Requirements Hampering Entry and Competition in the Steel Sector in Indonesia

In Indonesia, we know that there are issues related to the registration requirement for standards on steel bars and rods. Indeed, the data show that products in Harmonized System (HS) code 721310 (steel bars and rods) are subject to three NTMs and a measure for licensing linked with local production (E130) (figure 5.2). Two non-tariff measures pertain to this issue: product registration requirements (B810) and registration requirements for importers for reasons of technical barriers to trade (TBT) (B150).

To estimate if these NTMs have an impact on imports in the country, we employ price-based estimation of AVEs. Intuitively, it is a generalization of the well-known "price-gap" method recommended by annex V of the World Trade Organization (WTO) Agricultural Agreement. We use econometric estimation to decompose observed unit values into (a) a fraction that is explained by control variables and the average effect of our policy variable (the imposition of nontariff measures) and (b) a fraction that is driven by unobserved effects at the country-product level, including enforcement issues in particular. Enforcement is where NTMs that are being used as non-tariff barriers (NTBs) can be caught.

Formally, let e_{odp} designate residuals from equation (3.5) in chapter 3 and let $f^d(e_{odp})$ be their distribution for destination (importing) country d. Our indicator for identifying NTMs administered or designed as NTBs is the position of e_{odp} in the distribution of residuals for country d, $f^d(e_{odp})$. We propose to match evidence on the ground with econometric evidence of "unusually high" unit values, once those values have been purged of all observable influences, as shown in figure 5.1.

The average residuals for Indonesian imports of steel bars and rods are very high, creating hurdles for trade partners affected by these measures (figure 5.2).

Breaking down the distribution of unit value residuals for Indonesia's imports from China versus all partners, the position of HS 721310 from China is even more extreme when compared with that of other imports from China (figure 5.3, panel b). The distribution of residuals for each pair and each product shows that the residuals for Indonesia's imports of steel bar are higher for imports from China than for imports from other countries, constituting a major hurdle for Chinese firms seeking to enter the Indonesian market.

Figure 5.4 looks at all of the other exporters of steel bars and rods to Indonesia (all of which are from East Asia), showing that the restrictiveness of exports to Indonesia is targeted to specifically hurt Chinese exporters to Indonesia.

This highlights a very important policy issue. Our estimates suggest that the monopoly rents created by Indonesia's non-tariff barriers in steel are appropriated, at least partially, by traders from exporting countries (such as, China),

Figure 5.1 Decomposition of the Variation in Unit Values across Products and Country Pairs

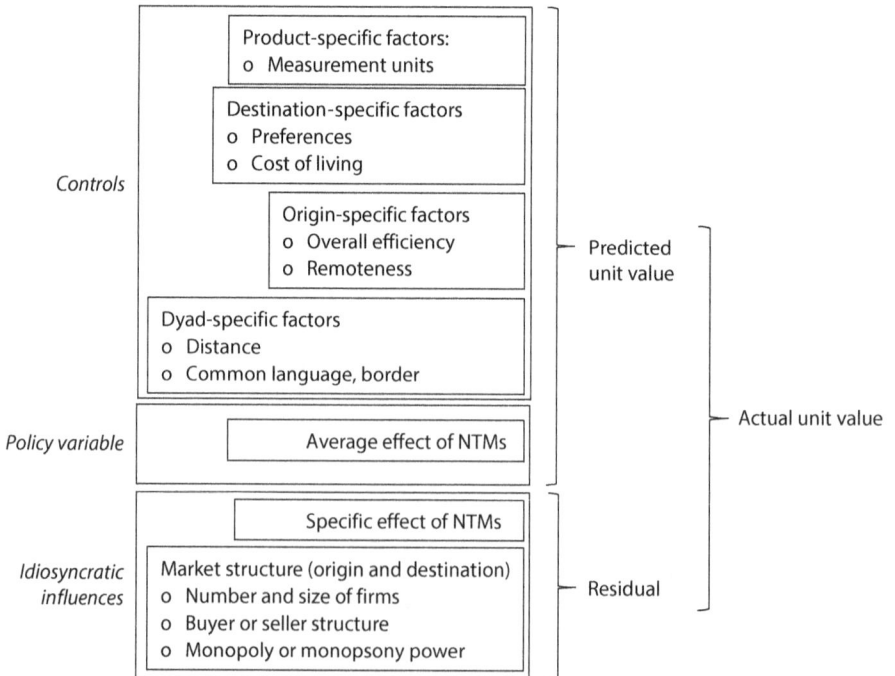

Note: NTM = non-tariff measure.

Figure 5.2 Distribution of Unit Value Residuals and Relative Position of Imported Steel Bars and Rods (Harmonized System 721310) in Indonesia

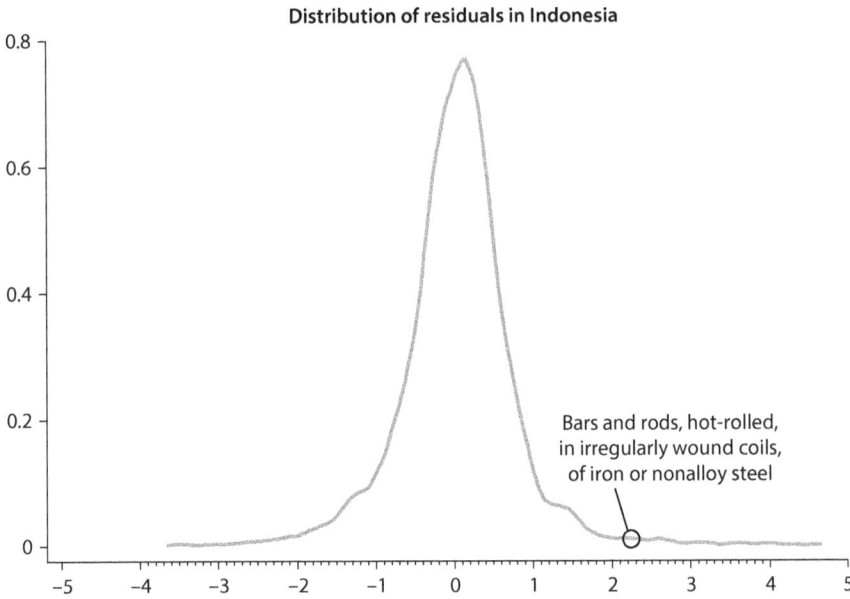

Distribution of residuals in Indonesia

Bars and rods, hot-rolled, in irregularly wound coils, of iron or nonalloy steel

Figure 5.3 Relative Position of Imported Steel Bars and Rods (Harmonized System 721310) in the Distribution of Unit Value Residuals in Indonesia, by Origin

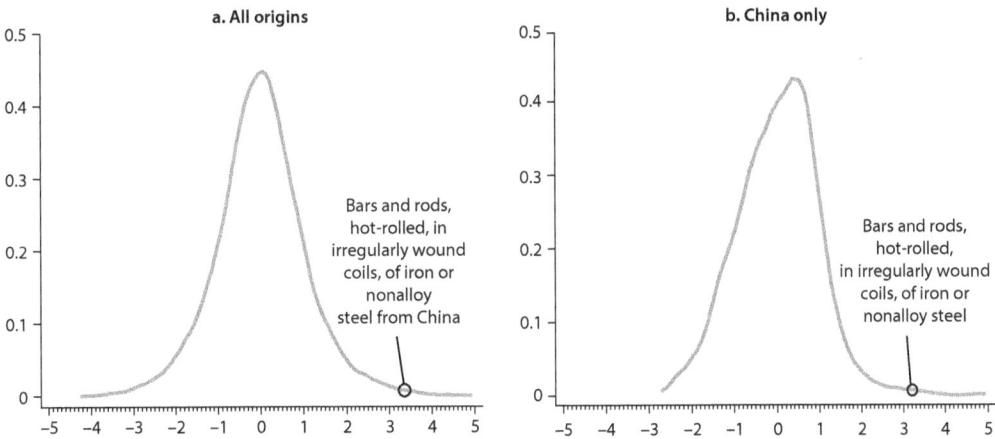

a. All origins

Bars and rods, hot-rolled, in irregularly wound coils, of iron or nonalloy steel from China

b. China only

Bars and rods, hot-rolled, in irregularly wound coils, of iron or nonalloy steel

since they are reflected in trade unit values. This may help to explain the lack of progress in negotiations to eliminate NTBs. If traders in exporting countries have their cut in the "protectionist loot," their governments will not push forcefully for the elimination of NTBs at the negotiating table. Who are the real losers? They are not Indonesia's trading partners. They are downstream buyers of steel bar *in Indonesia*.

Figure 5.4 Unit Value Residuals for Imported Steel Bars and Rods (Harmonized System 721310) in Indonesia, by Country of Origin

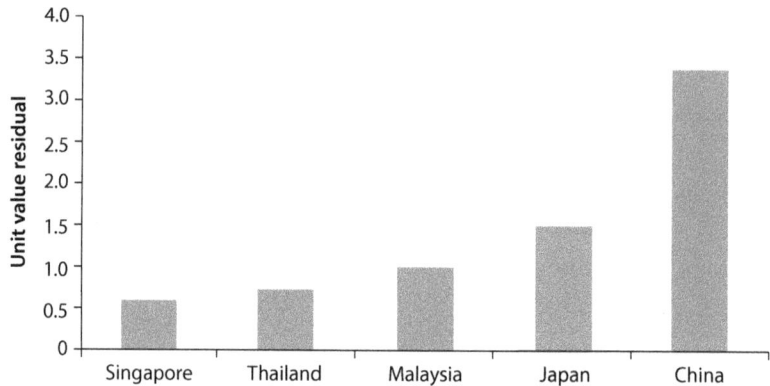

Thus, the Indonesian government should not consider the elimination of NTBs as a concession to its trading partners: it should consider this elimination as part of a pro-competitive agenda of regulatory improvement. Indeed, this is the key message of the World Bank's NTM Streamlining Toolkit (Cadot, Malouche, and Sáez 2012). Our quantitative analysis shows why making NTM streamlining part of national "better regulations" agendas is likely to be more promising than the current "identify-negotiate-eliminate" approach at the regional level.

Moreover, Indonesia's NTBs on imported steel affect not only China. As figure 5.4 shows, unit value residuals are also high on steel imports from Japan and Malaysia. In that case, NTBs are being directed at several trading partners, so their elimination is a public good for which it is unlikely that a working coalition can be built (as the stakes are low for Japan and Malaysia). This further undermines the "trade negotiations" approach to eliminating NTBs, reinforcing the point that the focus should shift to domestic regulatory improvement agendas.

We have used the case of steel in Indonesia to illustrate the back-and-forth process between systematic econometric analysis and case study analysis on the ground. We believe that this approach can deliver substantial understanding of the trade effects of NTMs. Econometric analysis *alone* is unlikely to yield a systematic way of identifying the use of NTMs as NTBs; finding, verifying, and understanding the facts on the ground are indispensable to understanding what special interests are at stake and what lobbying lineup has produced the observed policy distortion. Likewise, case studies and complaints originating from the private sector are unlikely, by themselves, to provide sufficient evidence for use in policy dialogue, because complaints are often riddled with disinformation and distorted facts. Thus, econometric analysis and case studies should be used jointly as reality checks on one another to provide a rich yet rigorous picture of regulatory distortions.

Export Registration Requirements and Mandatory Certificates of Origin Increase the Cost of Exports in Cambodia

Fixed Costs to Export: The Case of Cambodia

One of the main pillars of the Cambodian government's trade strategy for 2013–18 is to increase the competitiveness of Cambodian exports in world markets by strengthening the export business environment. In its effort to enhance the business environment, increase trade flows, and comply with the country's obligations under the Association of Southeast Asian Nations (ASEAN) Economic Community, the Cambodian government has embarked on a work program that includes the collection, classification, notification, and streamlining of NTMs in order to improve the country's trade performance and create new and better jobs.[1]

Export-Related Measures

Export-related measures are any type of legislation that the government of the exporting country applies on exported goods. They range from quantitative restrictions such as licenses, quotas, and prohibitions to the obligation to use state-trading enterprises for marketing and commercialization purposes. Countries differ in the way they apply and administer these measures worldwide.

How do export-related measures work in Cambodia? Favorable market access conditions accorded under preferential trade agreements remain conditional on rules of origin.[2] In Cambodia, the duty-free access that the country enjoys to the European Union (EU), China, Japan, and the Republic of Korea is the key element explaining the country's admirable recent export performance in the manufacturing industry. The garment and bicycle sectors have benefited prominently from this preferential market access. The United States, the second most important export destination, does not give Cambodia preferential market access.

Up to the end of 2013, firms in Cambodia had to be registered with the Ministry of Commerce (MoC) to be eligible to obtain a certificate of origin (CO) and export goods. This annual registration requirement costs around US$200, but much higher payments—up to US$800—have been reported. This large variation is explained by the informality of payments, which are often collected by brokers and mediators who contribute to the lack of cost transparency. In addition, Cambodian exporters have to obtain a certificate of origin for every single shipment, regardless of the treatment of their consignment in the destination market (preferential or most-favored nation). The official CO fee varies from a minimum of US$23 to a maximum of US$58, according to the type of certificate requested, the destination country, the size of shipment, and the type of products. Moreover, an export management fee applies to garment exports, depending on the destination. Businesses reportedly have to pay about US$30. The total CO cost is in the range of US$150–US$200, including brokers' fees. Reportedly about 150,000 COs are issued annually, at a total cost to exporters of US$22 million to US$30 million (3–4 percent of the total value of exports in 2011).

These measures significantly increase the cost for firms to engage in international trade and have a strong impact on the competitiveness of Cambodian exports and especially on the ability of small and medium enterprises (SMEs) to export, particularly in the handicraft and silk sectors. Only the most productive firms (larger enterprises) can afford to comply with these onerous regulations and maintain their profitability. Smaller firms either have to export informally— that is, ship small parcels without COs—or have to avoid export activity altogether.

How do export registration requirements work in other countries? Many countries use export registration requirements as well as certificates of origin. However, most countries administer them differently than Cambodia. Figure 5.5 provides a snapshot of the frequency ratio (share of products) and coverage ratio (export value) of export licenses in countries that report using this measure. Out of the 49 countries for which NTM data have been collected, 13 report using mandatory export registrations or licenses. However, only Sri Lanka applies them to all types of products. Other countries require export registrations only for specific sectors, such as minerals, metals, and garments.

How do registration requirements affect trade competitiveness? Annually registration requirements and compulsory certificates of origin increase firms' cost to reach export markets. These requirements weaken the competitiveness of Cambodian exporters not only because monetary costs to export rise but also because the collection of payments is inefficient, imposing a time tax on exporters. Footwear exporters reported that up to two weeks of two clerical workers are necessary to prepare all of the paperwork requested to file a CO application for a single container!

Figure 5.5 Licensing or Permit Requirements to Export in Select Countries: Coverage and Frequency Ratios

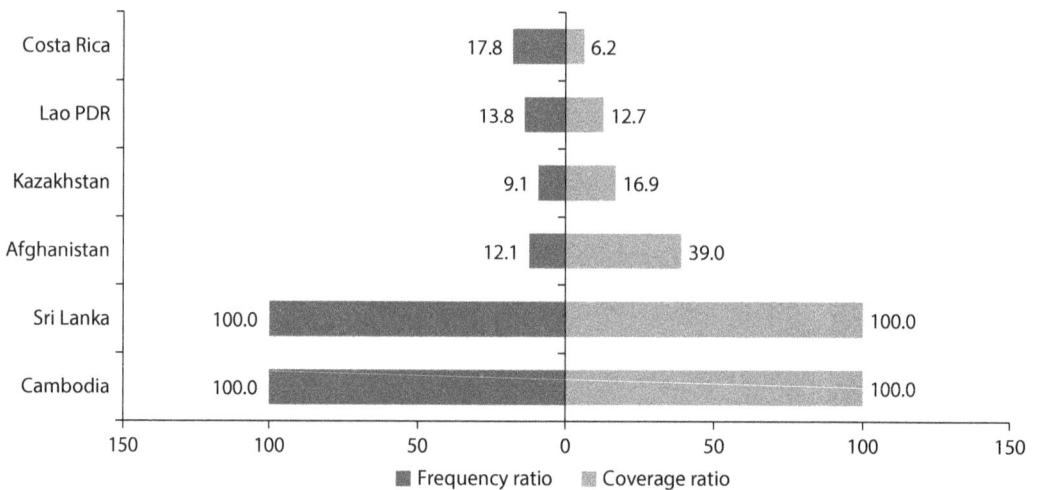

Source: Computation using the Global Non-Tariff Measures Database.
Note: The countries included are those that report using licensing or permit requirements to export (category P13 in the United Nations Conference on Trade and Development 2012 NTM classification) and for which the coverage ratio is larger than 5 percent. Countries not included that also use export licenses are Lebanon, Madagascar, Mauritius, Morocco, Nepal, Pakistan, and Tanzania. NTM = non-tariff measure.

The government justifies these measures on two grounds. First, the registration requirement allows it to ensure that companies applying for COs are active. Second, both the annual compulsory registration requirement and the CO allow the MoC to collect export statistics. Although these objectives are legitimate, the MoC could obtain the same results in a more cost-efficient way for the private sector. For example, checking the status of a company through the Tax Department and accessing export statistics through the automated customs system, which is managed by the General Department of Customs and Excise, would eliminate the need for costly mandatory export registrations.

Measuring the Impact of Export-Related Measures on Firms' Competitiveness: The Missing Middle

While mandatory registrations and certificates of origin increase the cost of doing business in Cambodia, little is known about their impact on the ability of firms to participate in international markets. We employ firm-level export data to show that few mid-size firms are able to export in Cambodia. We associate this low participation rate with large export costs, driven in part by export-related measures that disproportionally affect SMEs.

Using information from the World Bank Exporter Dynamics Database (EDD), figure 5.6 presents a scatterplot of the number of existing exporters (in logs) and

Figure 5.6 Number of Exporters and per Capita Income in Cambodia, 2009

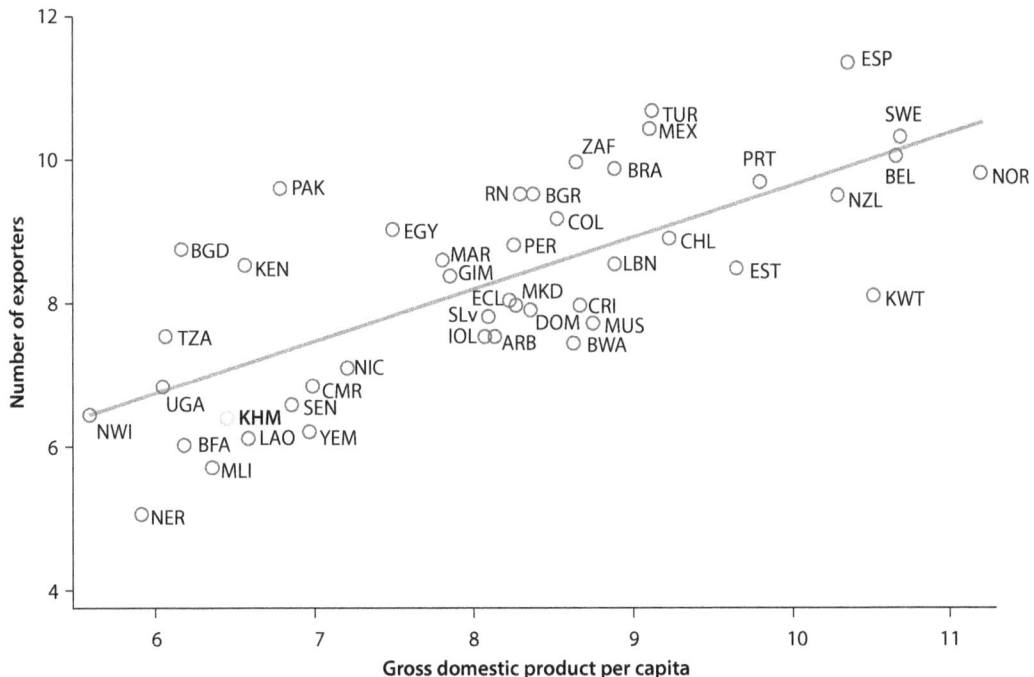

Source: Computation using the World Bank Exporters Dynamics Database.

Reforming Non-Tariff Measures • http://dx.doi.org/10.1596/978-1-4648-1138-8

the per capita gross domestic product (GDP) for all countries for which data are available.[3] Cambodia's number of exporters (around 600 in 2009) is lower than what is expected given its stage of development (solid line). In fact, the number of exporters in Cambodia is similar to that of Burkina Faso and Malawi, countries at a lower stage of development.

In Cambodia, very few medium-size enterprises are able to reach international markets. Well-established cross-country evidence indicates that few firms represent the lion's share of export value, while many SMEs account for a small part of a country's total export value. In other words, the distribution of export value across firms within a given country resembles a Pareto-shaped distribution.[4] Yet, this empirical regularity does not apply to Cambodia. Figure 5.7 plots the distribution of firm size in Cambodia in 2009 and compares it with that of Kenya and Pakistan, countries at similar levels of per capita income. The distribution of export value has a different shape in Cambodia than in the comparator countries. This asymmetric bimodal distribution implies that some small firms, very few mid-size firms, and relatively many large firms are involved in export. This finding suggests the presence of factors that discourage export activity for mid-size enterprises in Cambodia.

The shortage of mid-size exporters implies that, when we look at the aggregate pool of exporting firms, exporters from Cambodia are, on average, very different from exporters from similar countries. Cambodian firms are relatively larger, with a very low level of export concentration and a very high level of survival in international markets. All in all, Cambodia is an outlier among all countries for which firm-level export data are available. Figure 5.8 shows these

Figure 5.7 **Distribution of Export Value across Firms in Cambodia, 2009**

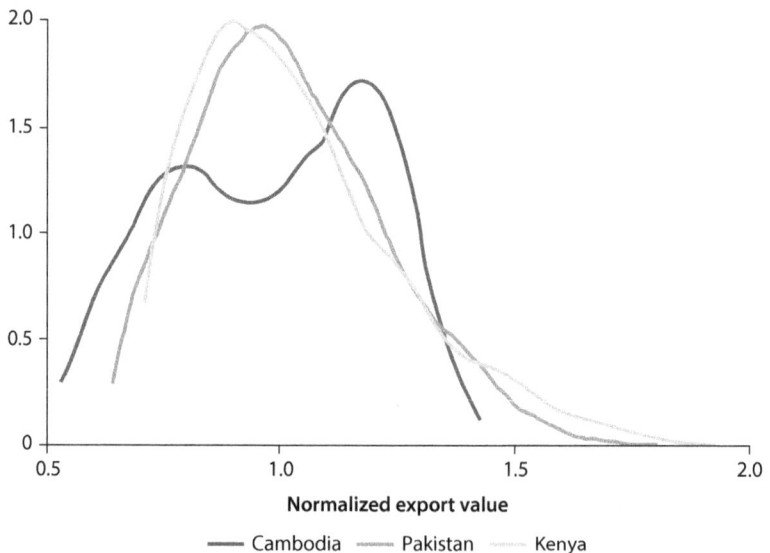

Source: Computation using the World Bank Export Dynamics Database.
Note: Export value is normalized by the median of each country distribution.

Reforming Non-Tariff Measures • http://dx.doi.org/10.1596/978-1-4648-1138-8

Figure 5.8 Export Size, Concentration, and Survival Rate of Firms, by Country 2009

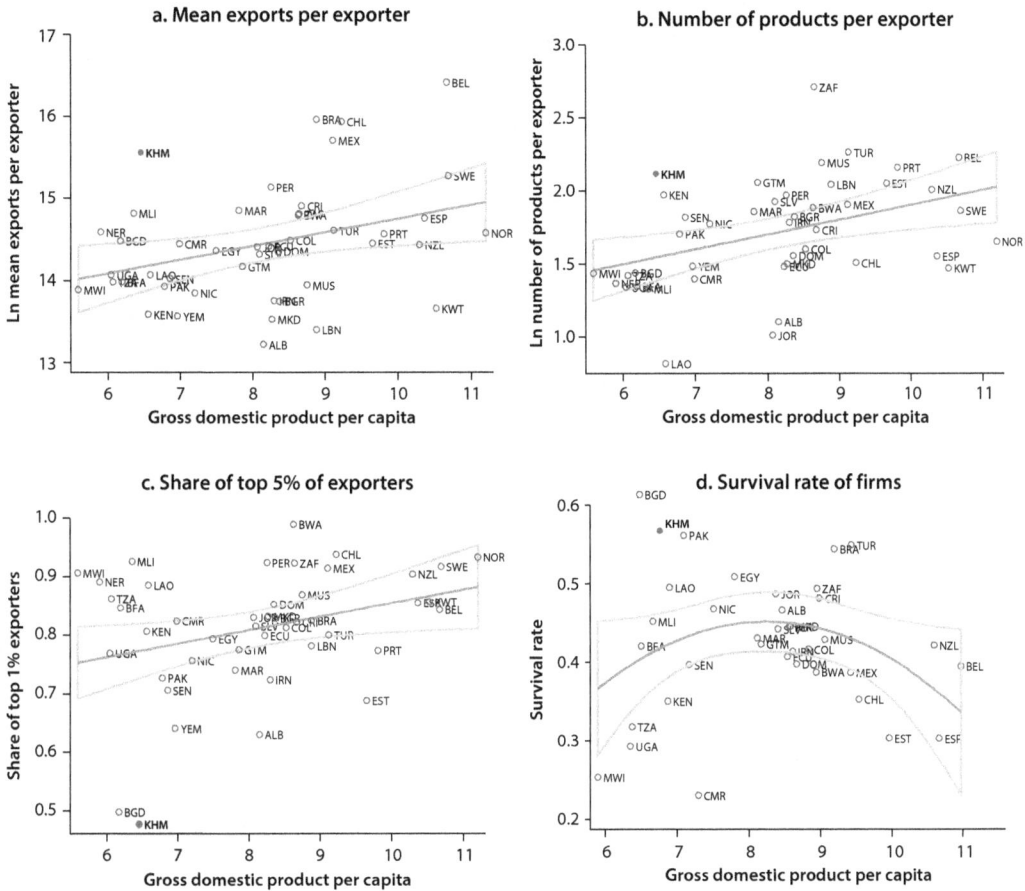

Source: Computation using the World Bank Enterprise Survey data.
Note: Ln = natural logarithm.

indicators for the set of countries available in the EDD. Panel a shows the mean export value per exporter, while panel b depicts the mean number of products per exporter. These two indicators are proxies for the size of exporters and indicate that Cambodian exporters are excessively large, on average, for the country's level of development. In fact, the average Cambodian firm exports an amount equivalent to that of Mexican exporters, but Cambodia's per capita GDP is only around 8 percent of Mexico's per capita GDP.

Cambodia's export value shows very low levels of concentration across firms. The top 5 percent of exporters (about 30 firms) account for around 45 percent of total export value (panel c). This level is exceptionally low by international standards: Cambodia has the lowest level of concentration among our set of countries. The predicted value of this indicator for a country like Cambodia is almost 80 percent. Additionally, Cambodian exporters display a remarkable rate of success in international markets (panel d). This indicator is computed as the number of firms that export in two consecutive years over the number of new entrants. Cambodia's firm survival rate is around 57 percent, again an outlier for its level of development. This implies that the number of new exporters in Cambodia each year is very small. A thriving export sector requires dynamic exporters testing new markets and products as well as new firms trying to become exporters. While some of these export tryouts succeed because they are profitable, others fail because they are not. The survival issue is a significant factor explaining differences in long-run export performance and is particularly important for low- and middle-income countries. In Cambodia, these patterns are not driven by cross-sectoral differences (box 5.1).

This review of the export dynamics of Cambodian firms with respect to similar countries provides three main results. First, Cambodia has a relatively low number of exporters. Second, those firms that export are mostly large; there are very few mid-size exporters. Third, these large exporters have a high rate of survival because very few firms are entering into export markets every year. These findings are consistent with the exceptionally large costs to export in Cambodia, which weaken the ability of medium-size firms, in particular, to participate in international trade. In the next section, we formally assess the role of Cambodia's specific trade costs in affecting the participation of firms in international markets.

Box 5.1 Are the Results Driven by Compositional Effects?

In order to check whether the aggregate patterns presented in figure 5.8 are affected by specific sectoral dynamics (that is, whether the garment sector, which is composed of very large enterprises, determines overall patterns), we ran a regression for each of our measures (size, number of products, share of top 5 percent of exporters, and survival rate) on a set of year, sector, and country fixed effects. A sector is a two-digit HS code, and the data are for 2002–09. The Cambodia country-specific fixed effect indicates whether the relationship between Cambodia and the average of other countries is significant, controlling for differences across countries, years, and economic sectors. Results presented in table B5.1.1 indicate that the patterns observed in figure 5.8 are not driven by sectoral dynamics. All Cambodia-specific country effects are statistically significant and have the expected sign.

Table B5.1.1 Size, Concentration, and Survival Rate of Export Firms in Cambodia

Size of firm	Exports per exporter	Number of products per exporter	Share of top 5% of exporters	Survival rate
Cambodia fixed effects	1.888***	0.036*	−0.012**	0.413***
	(0.135)	(0.022)	(0.052)	(0.067)
Year fixed effects	Yes	Yes	Yes	Yes
Country fixed effects	Yes	Yes	Yes	Yes
Sector fixed effects	Yes	Yes	Yes	Yes
Observations.	28,356	27,902	20,596	18,430
R^2	0.464	0.262	0.414	0.246

Source: Computations using information from the Exporter Dynamics Database.

Cambodian Export Costs in Regional Perspective

The literature on international trade has established that export participation is determined mostly by variable costs, such as transport costs and tariffs, and fixed export costs, such as market entry costs. This combination affects firm profitability and—given that firms differ in their level of productivity—also affects their ability to engage in exports. As a result, firms that are able to overcome the costs to export are usually the biggest and most productive firms within a country (Melitz 2003). There is, then, a direct relationship between the level of trade costs and the minimum productivity threshold required to export. The larger trade costs are, the more productive firms need to be in order to engage successfully in exports. Employing the World Bank Enterprise Surveys, we investigate the export productivity premium in five countries in the ASEAN region, including Cambodia.[5] We then estimate the size of country-specific export costs in those countries and assess their role in explaining the probability that a domestic firm decides to export. We pay particular attention to the impact of costs across firms of different sizes. The aim is to show that Cambodia's export dynamics are the result of excessively high trade costs in relation to costs in other countries in the region.

Around 24 percent of all firms in Cambodia are able to export (table 5.1). This is similar to other ASEAN countries for which data are available. Vietnam has the largest share of firms that are able to export (36 percent), while Indonesia has the lowest share (16 percent). Cambodia has the lowest share of mid-size firms that export (6 percent). Cambodia's share of small and large firms in export participation is comparable to that of the other countries. These findings confirm the missing middle phenomenon shown.

Firms that export in Cambodia and in other countries in the region are larger and more productive than firms that only serve the domestic market. Table 5.2 reports the median size of exporters and domestic firms in our sample of countries. It also reports two measures of firm productivity to compare the productivity of exporters versus nonexporters.[6] The median exporting firm in Cambodia employs 443 people, while the median nonexporting firm employs only 18 people. The difference in firm size proxied by employment between exporters and nonexporters in Cambodia is the largest in the region. Exporters are also more productive than nonexporters in both Cambodia and other countries in our sample.[7]

Table 5.1 Share of Exporters in Five Southeast Asian Countries, by Firm Size, 2009

	Cambodia	Indonesia	Lao PDR	Philippines	Vietnam
Small (<20)	3.8	1.2	0.6	5.7	6.9
Medium (20–99)	6.0	12.7	10.5	19.7	18.0
Large (100 and over)	50.3	51.5	46.2	44.7	55.1
Total	24.2	16.0	29.4	26.5	36.2

Source: Computation using the World Bank Enterprise Survey Database.
Note: Size is defined by the number of full-time employees declared by each firm. Information for Cambodia is for 2011. Information for the other countries is for 2009.

Table 5.2 Median Size and Productivity of Exporters in Five Southeast Asian Countries

Indicator	Cambodia	Indonesia	Lao PDR	Philippines	Vietnam
Size (employment)					
Exporters	443.5	280.0	211.5	95.5	170.0
Nonexporters	18.0	9.0	15.0	25.0	30.0
Labor productivity					
Exporters	1.02	1.07	0.98	1.01	1.01
Nonexporters	0.98	0.98	0.98	0.99	0.99
Total factor productivity					
Exporters	0.02	−0.11	−0.27	0.25	0.04
Nonexporters	−0.13	−0.05	−0.33	0.00	−0.06

Source: Computation using the World Bank Enterprise Survey Database.
Note: Size is the total number of permanent full-time employees. Labor productivity is the log difference between sales and employment. Total factor productivity corresponds to the standard Solow residual estimated from a Cobb-Douglass production function. Information for Cambodia is for 2011. Information for the other countries is for 2009.

Firms in Cambodia, unlike firms in other countries in the region, find it particularly difficult to engage in exports. We use the empirical model in appendix C to estimate the probability that domestic firms participate in export markets, by firm size, comparing Cambodia to other countries in the region. Results, depicted in figure 5.9, show that firms in Cambodia have the lowest estimated probability to export within our sample of countries. Large establishments have a 30 percent chance to export in Cambodia, compared with almost 50 percent in Vietnam. The same pattern is observed across all firm-size categories.

The very low probability to export in Cambodia is explained by excessively high export costs, which disincentivize firms' participation in international trade. Estimated export costs in each country, depicted in figure 5.10, are computed using the empirical model presented in appendix C. Export costs in Cambodia are around 40 percent higher than the regional average. They are the highest in our sample of countries and very similar to those in the Lao People's Democratic Republic, a non-WTO member for the year in which the data were collected. Consistent with the relatively high probability to export, Vietnam has the lowest trade costs in our sample.

Export costs are determined by country-specific factors that can be related, directly or indirectly, to trade. There is mounting evidence that firms wishing to export not only face variable costs, such as transport costs and external tariffs, but also—critically—fixed costs that do not vary with export volume, such as costs related to the domestic and foreign regulatory environment. We now decompose the main trade determinants underlying export costs in our sample of countries.

The number of documents needed to export and the logistics costs appear to be the most important factors hindering the ability to export of Cambodian firms (table 5.3). Eight documents are needed to export, which is the double the number required in Indonesia, and 22 days are needed to export a 20-foot container,

Figure 5.9 Estimated Probability to Export in Five Southeast Asian Countries, by Firm Size

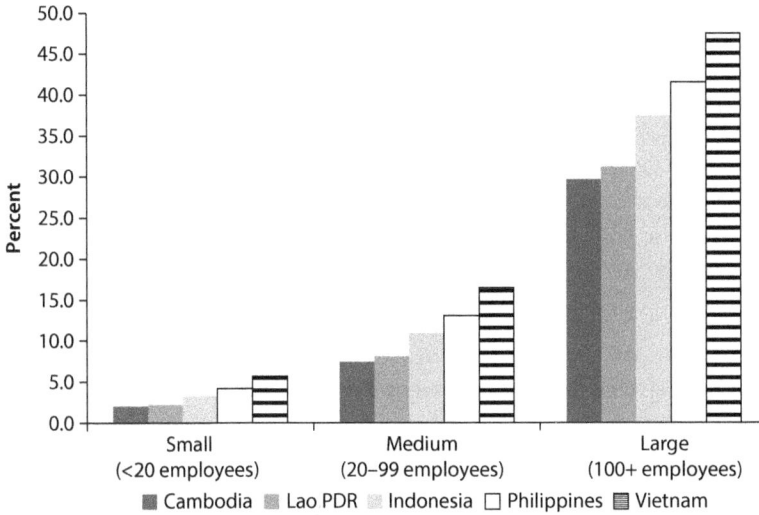

Source: Computation using the World Bank Enterprise Survey Database.
Note: Information for Cambodia is for 2011; information for the other countries is for 2009.

Figure 5.10 Estimated Fixed Costs to Export in Five Southeast Asian Countries

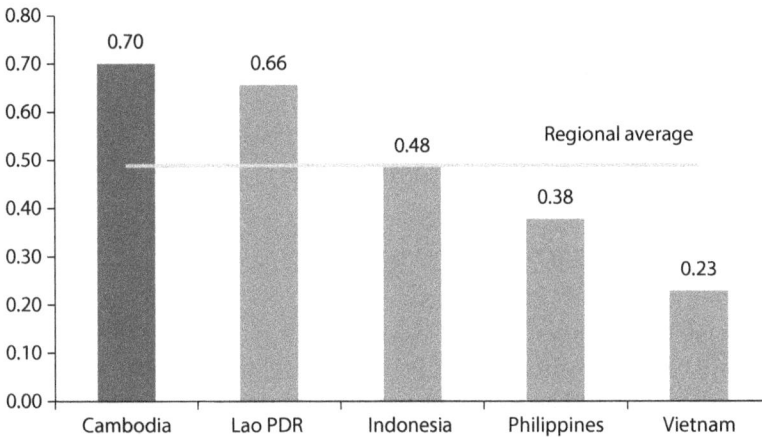

Source: Computation using the World Bank Enterprise Survey Database.

which is one of the longest times in the region.[8] In contrast, the country is well connected to international markets given its geographic location and the quality of its port infrastructure, which is ranked above the regional average.

The most burdensome export documents to comply with are export licenses and certifications of origin. Figure 5.11 shows the most burdensome NTMs by order of difficulty as reported by a firm survey conducted in 2013 by the

Table 5.3 Indicators of Trading across Borders in Five Southeast Asian Countries

	Cambodia	Indonesia	Lao PDR	Philippines	Vietnam
Logistic performance index 1–5 (worst to best)	2.6	2.9	2.5	3.0	3.0
Documents to export (number)	8.0	4.0	10.0	6.0	5.0
Time to export (days)	22.0	17.0	23.0	15.0	21.0
Cost to export (US$ per container)	795.0	615.0	1950.0	585.0	610.0
Burden of customs procedures 1–7 (worst to best)	3.9	4.0	—	3.2	3.4
Liner shipping connectivity index 0–100 (low to high)	3.5	26.3	—	17.2	48.7
Quality of port infrastructure 1–7 (worst to best)	4.2	3.6	—	3.3	3.4

Source: World Bank Trading Across Borders Database.
Note: The burden of customs procedures measures business executives' perceptions of the efficiency of their country's customs procedures.
The liner shipping connectivity index measures the cost to ship a priority express air package weighing 1 kilogram through DHL to the United
States. — = not available.

Figure 5.11 Burdensome Internal NTMs Faced by Exporters in Cambodia, 2013

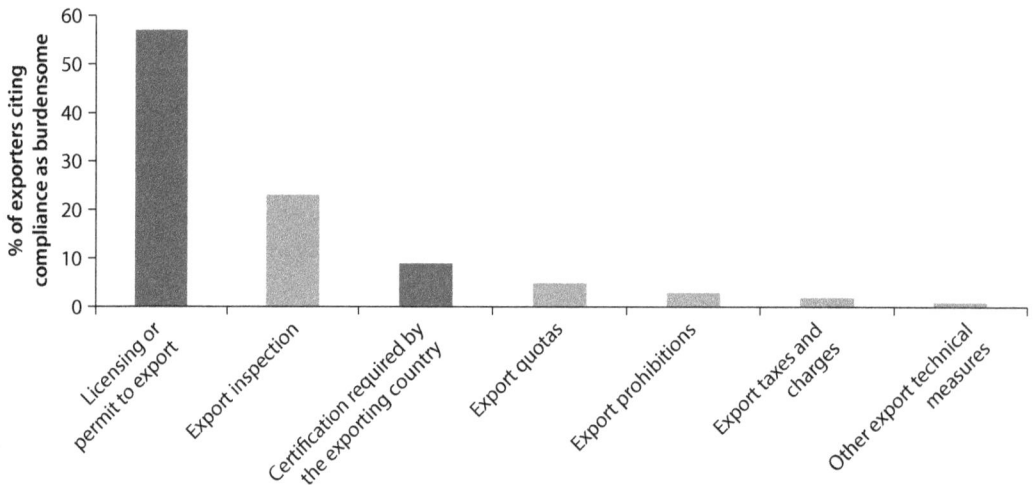

Source: International Trade Center and World Bank Enterprise Survey Database.

International Trade Center. Export registration requirements are considered the most complicated measure to comply with, followed by export inspection and certifications of origin. These two documents and the way they operate increase the cost to export for private firms in the country and weaken their ability to compete in international markets.

We have used the case of export requirements in Cambodia to illustrate the impact of poorly written regulations that harms the competitiveness of exporters.

In November 2013, the Cambodian government enacted policy actions aimed at streamlining these measures. The MoC removed the obligation to register annually. Additionally, traders can now request a certificate of origin only when it is required by their trading partner to obtain preferential treatment. By reducing the cost to export, these policies are expected to have a substantial impact on firm participation, mainly for mid-size firms.

Export Bans Impact the Poor in Nigeria

Nigeria prohibits the import of a wide range of 27 groups of products, listed in table 5.4. Some of those products can be considered necessities, such as those under category 26 (which includes exercise books and pencils) or category 9 (which includes common pain killers such as aspirin and paracetamol).

In general, import bans raise the domestic price of prohibited products to the point where domestic supply meets domestic demand. In Nigeria, unknown quantities may be smuggled into the country via a porous border with Benin. Little is known about the quantities involved and the cost of smuggling, so this hidden import supply cannot be estimated directly. What is clear, however, is that smuggling cannot completely fill the vacuum created by the import ban and is likely to involve costs. Thus, quantities available on the Nigerian domestic market are likely to be restricted, and prices are likely to be higher than without the ban. This has three effects. It raises the rents accruing to domestic producers, raises the cost of living, and reduces the welfare of domestic consumers. In addition, the ban can have distributional effects. First, if the prohibited goods are inferior ones, the ban is regressive, meaning that it affects the poor more than the rich;

Table 5.4 Products Subject to Import Bans in Nigeria

Category	Product
1	Live or dead birds (including frozen poultry)
2	Pork, beef, mutton, lamb, goat meat
3	Bird eggs
4	Vegetables oils and fats
5	Spaghetti noodles
6	Fruit juices in retail packs
7	Water
8	Bagged cement
9	Medicine and medical supplies
10	Pharmaceuticals waste
11	Finished soaps and detergent
12	Mosquito coils
13	Sanitary plastic ware
14	Toothpicks
15	Rethreaded and used tires
16	Corrugated paper and paper board
17	Toilet paper
18	Textiles and fabrics
19	All types of footwear and bags
20	Hollow glass bottles
21	Used compressors, air conditioners, and refrigerators or freezers
22	Furniture
23	Certain electric-generating items
24	Ballpoint pens
25	Telephone recharge cards

if the prohibited goods are superior ones, the ban affects the rich more than the poor. Second, if smuggling is more difficult in remote regions, the quantity-constraining effect of the ban is higher in those regions.

Replacing import bans with tariffs generally has several effects, each of which depends on the rate of tariff chosen to replace the ban. If the rate is set to maintain the domestic price constant, the only effect is to generate tariff revenue for the government. If the rate is set at a lower level, the tariff has three effects:

- It reduces the rents accruing to domestic producers.
- It reduces the cost of living and raises the welfare of domestic consumers.
- It raises government tariff revenue.

In this section, we estimate the second of these effects in three steps, each consisting of multiple substeps.

First, we estimate AVEs for the prohibitions, product by product. That is, we calculate the rate of tariffs that would leave domestic prices constant. For this, we use price data provided by the Economist Intelligence Unit (EIU) for Lagos and comparator cities (Nairobi and Douala). Our price-gap estimates are calculated in a way that filters out general differences in the cost of living between Lagos and comparator cities. We then adjust our price estimates by state, using price data from the National Bureau of Statistics, in order to take into account regional price differences within Nigeria. Price data are provided in appendix D.

Second, we estimate the share of each prohibited product in household expenditure, using data from Nigeria's household expenditure survey. This involves matching product classifications between the EIU, the National Bureau of Statistics' price data, and the household survey.

Third, we simulate alternative scenarios concerning the elimination of prohibitions or their replacement by tariffs.

Food items represent a very large share of household expenditure, and the share of those products affected by import bans is substantial. At the national level, average expenditure on food items represents 65.37 percent of total household expenditure. Roughly 13–15 percent of that expenditure is on products affected by the current import prohibitions. As for nonfood items, nearly 10 percent of household expenditure is affected by the bans (aggregating frequent and less frequent items).

The share of products affected by the import bans varies slightly across Nigeria's regions, although differences are moderate. As shown in table 5.5, expenditure patterns in the north are slightly skewed in favor of the products affected by import bans compared with patterns in the south, accounting for 26 and 21 percent of household expenditure, respectively. The western zone seems less affected than the eastern and central zones, but the difference is not very large.

Table 5.6 shows differences in the basket of commodities consumed by the 25 percent poorest and the 25 percent richest. However, there is apparently no systematic difference in the share of products affected by import bans across

Table 5.5 Household Expenditure Patterns in Nigeria, by Region

Item	National	North-central	Northeast	Northwest	South-central	Southeast	Southwest
Food							
Total food items	65.37	64.49	63.45	65.68	64.47	68.97	64.63
Food items under bans	13.47	14.64	15.69	14.28	13.31	12.22	11.16
Staples	5.73	7.57	7.09	6.78	5.81	4.54	5.02
Meat	6.23	6.53	8.46	7.38	6.06	6.78	5.49
Beverage	0.64	0.53	0.22	0.17	1.16	0.97	0.67
Nonfood frequent							
Total frequent items	24.76	24.56	24.77	22.84	26.6	23.7	26.14
Frequent items under bans	4.31	4.59	5.49	4.65	4.03	4.19	3.1
Household supplies	3.13	3.85	4.66	3.92	2.52	2.29	1.89
Medicine and medical supplies	0.91	0.49	0.52	0.41	1.30	1.68	0.91
Nonfood less frequent							
Total less frequent items	9.87	10.95	11.78	11.48	8.93	7.33	9.23
Less frequent under bans	5.42	5.72	6.53	6.4	4.84	3.8	5.26
Textile and clothing	5.13	5.46	6.00	5.79	4.27	3.56	5.11
Air conditioner and refrigerator or freezer	0.13	0.09	0.10	0.28	0.15	0.04	0.06
Total under bans	23.2	24.95	27.71	25.33	22.18	20.21	19.52

Table 5.6 Household Expenditure Patterns in Nigeria, by Income Quartile

Item	National	Q1	Q2	Q3	Q5
Food					
Total food items	65.37	71.17	68.5	66.11	60.58
Food items under bans	13.47	14.19	13.79	13.43	13.01
Staples	5.73	6.60	5.97	4.75	5.14
Meat	6.23	6.94	6.87	6.60	6.72
Beverage	0.64	0.40	0.62	0.67	0.72
Nonfood frequent					
Total frequent items	24.76	21.18	23.17	24.42	27.44
Frequent items under bans	4.31	4.84	4.58	4.24	3.70
Household supplies	3.13	3.97	3.64	3.20	2.43
Medicine and medical supplies	0.91	0.84	0.88	0.99	0.90
Nonfood less frequent					
Total less frequent items	9.87	7.65	8.34	9.47	11.97
Less frequent under bans	5.42	5.61	6.02	6.3	7.29
Textile and clothing	5.13	4.61	4.86	5.05	5.56
Air conditioner and refrigerator or freezer	0.13	0.01	0.03	0.04	0.29
Total under bans	23.2	24.64	24.39	23.97	24

Source: Nigerian household survey.

income groups: the share of banned products is around 23 percent at all income
levels. This means that the bans are not specifically regressive or progressive on
the basis of expenditure patterns.

We now outline the broader effects of the elimination of the import bans on
both consumers and producers.

Import prohibitions can be imposed for two main reasons:

- To discourage the consumption or industrial use of products that are detri-
  mental to societal welfare
- To protect domestic producers of prohibited products from outside competition.

In the first case, the justification is based on what economists call a *negative
externality* linked to use of the products. Examples include toxic chemicals or
pesticides. The prohibition should cover any *sale* of the product, whether
imported or produced locally. A prohibition on imports alone cannot be an ade-
quate instrument to protect society from negative consumption or intermediate-
use externalities. As a practical matter, in the case of Nigeria's prohibited
products, none seems to be dangerous or harmful. It is hard to see the downside
of using toothpicks or wheelbarrows, and products like exercise books, pens, or
pain killers are associated with *positive* consumption externalities.

In the second case, the justification is based on the reasoning that the higher
domestic price generated by the prohibition will encourage domestic production.
However, the actual encouragement of domestic production will depend on the
domestic market structure. When the domestic market is competitive, domestic
production is encouraged. When it is not, the production-encouragement effect
is smaller and can even be almost nonexistent, leaving only deadweight losses.
Conversely, eliminating the prohibition will reduce production under competition, but may have smaller or nonexistent effects on domestic production if there
is domestic market power. We show why with the help of two diagrams.

Figure 5.12 shows the effect of the elimination of bans when the domestic
market structure is competitive. When the import prohibition is enforced, the
domestic price settles at the intersection of the domestic supply and demand
curves, which is the upper horizontal curve. If the prohibition is lifted and
replaced by free trade, the domestic price shrinks to the world price (inclusive of
all trade costs), which is the lower horizontal line. The height between the two
lines is the prohibition's AVE, which we estimate using the price-gap method.
The shared area represents the gains generated for consumers by the prohibition's elimination. It is made up of two components: the part to the left of the
domestic supply curve is a transfer from producers (what used to be profits for
domestic producers becomes welfare for consumers), and the part to the right of
the domestic supply curve corresponds to the elimination of the so-called deadweight losses created by the prohibition. It can be thought of as the sum of a
rectangle whose area is the product of the AVE (the height) times quantities
consumed under the prohibition regime (the base) and a right-angle triangle
whose area is half the AVE (the height) times the increase in consumption

Figure 5.12 Effect of an Import Prohibition When the Domestic Market Structure Is Competitive

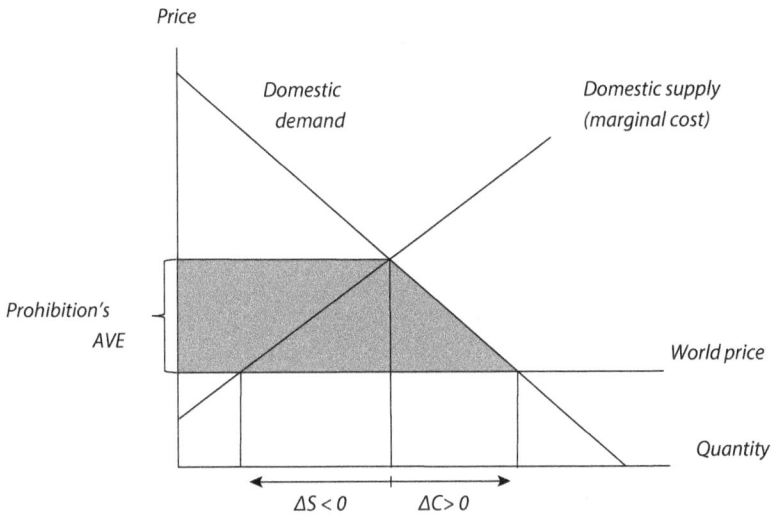

expected after elimination of the prohibition. This approach is how we estimate the welfare gain from the prohibition's elimination.

When there is domestic production, as we have assumed here, producers will see their sales and profits shrink after the prohibition's elimination; as a result, they will reduce production and employment. This effect is shown by the left-pointing arrow at the bottom of figure 5.12. When the domestic market structure is not competitive, the prohibition elimination's effect is quite different, as shown in figure 5.13.

The analysis is qualitatively similar, except that we now assume a single domestic producer. The prohibition grants this producer monopoly power, which he uses not to expand output, but to raise prices. This can be seen by the fact that even though the domestic demand curves are exactly identical in figures 5.12 and 5.13, in figure 5.13 the domestic price settles at a higher level and domestic output is lower. This is a key point: quantitative restrictions and prohibitions hand monopoly power to domestic producers that they use not to create employment but to raise prices. Therefore, quantitatively, the effect of the prohibition's elimination differs from that shown in figure 5.12 in two ways:

- The price reduction is larger, so *consumers gain more*. In particular, the deadweight losses removed by the prohibition's elimination (the triangular area under the demand curve) are larger.
- The reduction of domestic output is lower, so *employment suffers less*. This is visible in figure 5.13 through the dashed apparent supply curve, which shows a large price reduction (the prohibition's AVE) triggering only a small output reduction, *as if* supply is inelastic. In fact, it is not that supply is inelastic

Figure 5.13 Effect of an Import Prohibition When the Domestic Market Structure Is a Monopoly

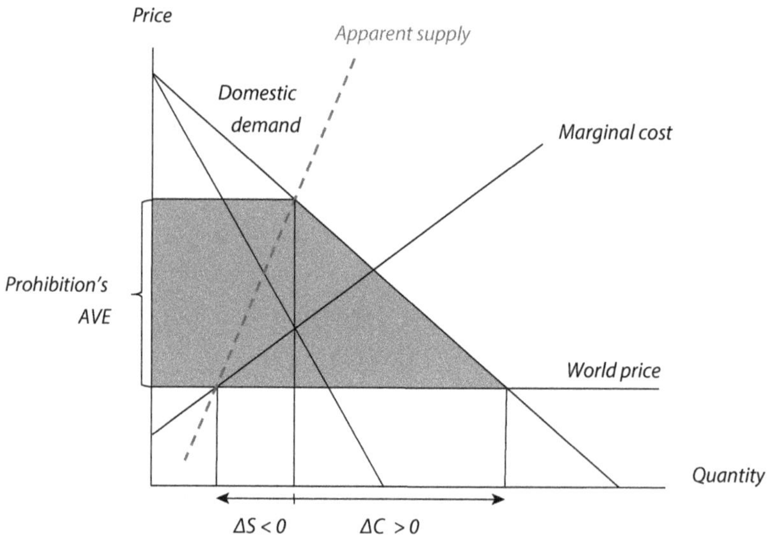

(marginal cost curves are the same in figures 5.12 and 5.13); rather, it is that phasing out the prohibition strips the domestic producer of his monopoly power.

If there were a handful of producers (an *oligopoly*), the situation could not be depicted graphically and would be somewhere between figures 5.12 and 5.13. Only in the extreme case of pure and perfect competition (an unlikely market structure in a low- and middle-income country) would the output-reduction effect of the prohibition's elimination be strictly proportional to the elasticity of supply.

This analysis has two implications for simulation analysis when the domestic market structure is less than perfectly competitive:

- When simulating the output-reduction effect of the prohibition's phaseout, it is reasonable and legitimate to assume a very low apparent elasticity of supply (corresponding to the dashed line in figure 5.13).
- When simulating the demand-increasing effect of the prohibition's phaseout, it is also reasonable and legitimate to assume a larger-than-1 elasticity of demand, because a domestic monopoly would never operate in the inelastic part of the demand curve.

Both assumptions highlight the beneficial effects of the prohibition's phase-out. We use the second in the simulations reported in the next section.

Estimating the Impact of Import Bans on Domestic Prices

In annex V of the Agricultural Agreement, the WTO recommends using price gaps to calculate the AVE of NTMs.[9] The price gap for a product affected by an NTM such as a prohibition is the difference between its domestic price and the counterfactual price that would obtain in the absence of the NTM. Of course, the counterfactual is not apparent, so approximations must be used. The WTO recommends using the cost, insurance, freight price of the same good in a similar market not affected by NTMs. The choice of a similar market is a matter of judgment, involving comparisons of size, proximity, transport costs, domestic market structure, income level, and—most important of all— data availability.

For the products concerned by Nigeria's prohibition phaseouts, we use prices published by the EIU for a basket of consumption goods observed in the world's largest cities. The formula for the price gap for product k in country i is simply

$$g_k^i = \frac{p_k^i - p_k^c}{p_k^c},\tag{5.1}$$

where c stands for a comparator, either a country or a basket of countries (in which case p_k^c is an average price in the comparators).

We use a slightly more sophisticated formula that takes into account systematic differences in the cost of living between Nigeria and the comparator countries. That is, suppose that the price gap for a prohibited product is 20 percent, but consumption goods not affected by NTMs are, on average, 5 percent more expensive at home than in the comparator country. Then the relevant price gap should be only 15 percent. To take this difference into account, we first calculate the simple average[10] of price gaps for all goods outside of the list of prohibitions:

$$g^{-i} = \frac{1}{N} \sum_{m \neq k} \frac{p_m^i - p_m^c}{p_m^c}.\tag{5.2}$$

The effective price gap is then

$$\tilde{g}_k^i = \frac{g_k^i - g^{-i}}{1 + g^{-i}}.\tag{5.3}$$

In the case of Nigeria's prohibitions, we have used Nairobi as comparator city for Lagos.[11] Price comparisons by aggregates, presented in table 5.7, show that, as expected, price gaps are systematically larger for banned products than for other products. For banned products, the simple average is a whopping 92 percent. For other products, it is 15 percent, which is our estimate of g^{-i}. That is, we subtract 15 percent from the banned products' observed price gaps in order to correct for general cost-of-living differences between Lagos and Nairobi. This leaves an average price gap of $92 - 15 = 77$ percent for banned products (see appendix D for detailed price gaps by products).

Reforming Non-Tariff Measures • http://dx.doi.org/10.1596/978-1-4648-1138-8

Table 5.7 Price-Gap Calculations for Lagos versus Nairobi
Price index (Lagos = 100)

Product	Staples	Protein	Beverages	Household supplies	Personal care products	Total
Banned products	178	30	−7	67	194	92
Other	61	−24	−26	−12	−17	15

Source: Calculations of the Economist Intelligence Unit.

Figure 5.14 Price Levels in Nigeria, by Cluster and Region

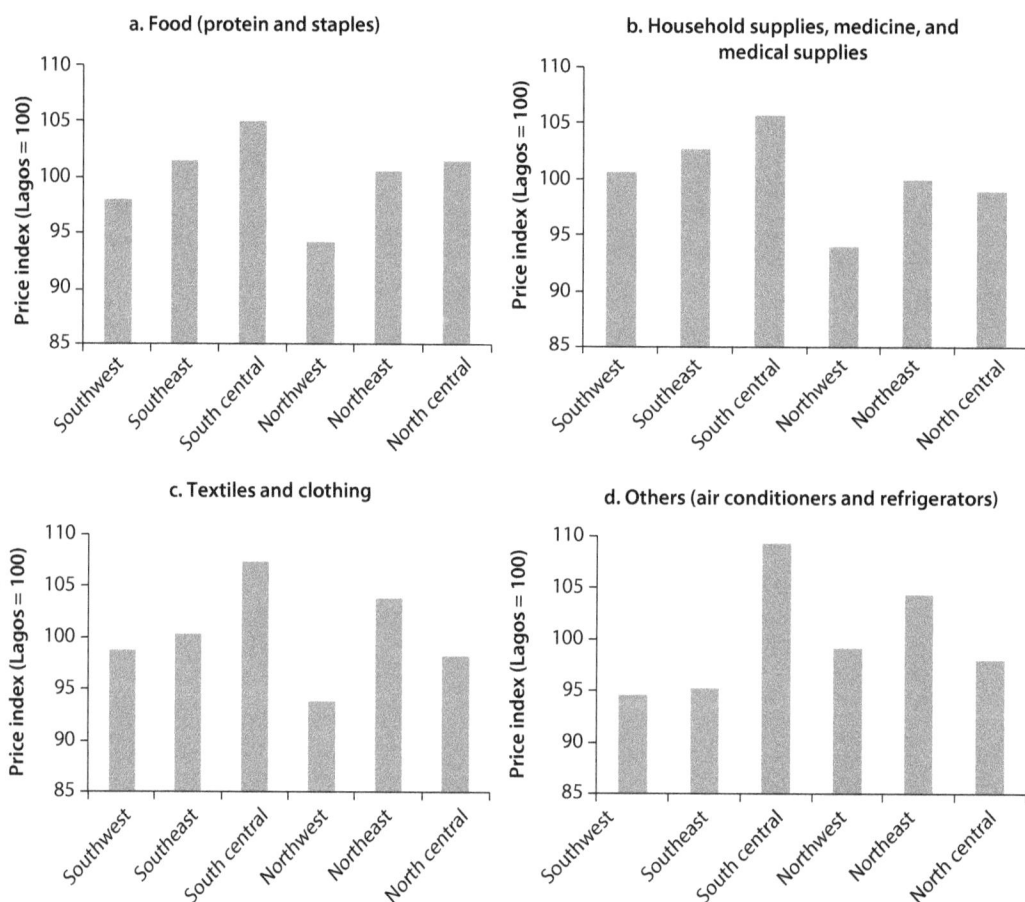

a. Food (protein and staples)

b. Household supplies, medicine, and medical supplies

c. Textiles and clothing

d. Others (air conditioners and refrigerators)

The price-gap approach can also be used to estimate the impact of removing import prohibitions across the country. Since prohibited goods are obtainable in practice through smuggling, we might also observe a price gap between cities close to the Beninese border and cities far from the border. We then adjust our price estimates by zones, using price data from the National Bureau of Statistics, in order to take into account price differences among Nigerian regions.

In general, prices are higher in provinces other than the western ones. This is illustrated in figure 5.14, which shows regional prices for selected groups of products (Lagos = 100).

Figure 5.15 Price Levels of Banned and Other Products in Nigeria, by Region
Price index (Lagos = 100)

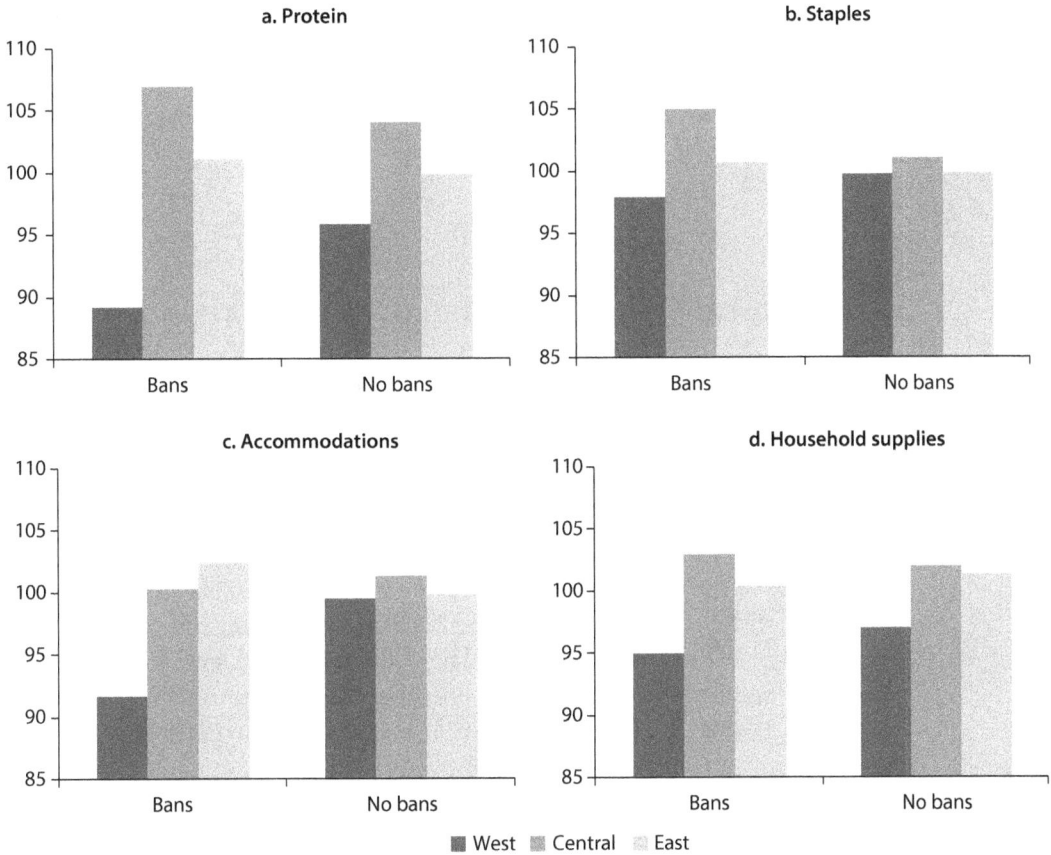

a. Protein

b. Staples

c. Accommodations

d. Household supplies

■ West ▨ Central ▨ East

The same cross-regional pattern of prices holds, qualitatively, for banned and for other products. However, the bans seem to magnify price dispersion between western and other provinces, as shown in figure 5.15 across all product clusters. Thus, the presence of the bans magnifies transportation-cost differences across regions, perhaps because they force traders to import using roundabout routes (either smuggling or importing in small quantities to avoid the "commercial" categorization).

Simulating the Welfare Impact of Eliminating the Import Bans

The items slated for elimination of import prohibitions are narrowly defined and mostly consumption goods. Therefore, general-equilibrium analysis would likely suffer from aggregation bias and would, compared with partial-equilibrium analysis, pick up effects of secondary importance. Partial-equilibrium analysis at a disaggregated level is more appropriate, and it is the route we take. We assume that preferences are quasi-linear, which implies that changes in welfare are equivalent to changes in real income, and use the two terms interchangeably.

We now calculate the gains to Nigerian consumers accruing from the selective elimination of import prohibitions on the goods appearing in appendix D. We ignore the issue of transfers from domestic producers to consumers and calculate the effect of the whole price reduction, which is the sum of the price reduction on baseline consumption of hitherto prohibited products and the added welfare brought about by the induced increase in consumption. That is,

$$\Delta W = \Sigma_k E_k^0 \left[\Delta pk + \frac{1}{2} \varepsilon_k (\Delta p_k)^2 \right], \tag{5.4}$$

where k is the prohibited products, E_K^0 is baseline expenditure on good k, Δp_k is the price gap for good k, and ε is the price elasticity of demand (*in absolute value*). Using the AVE of the price gap, the formula becomes

$$\Delta W = \Sigma_k E_K^0 \left[\frac{t_k}{1+t_k} + \frac{1}{2} \varepsilon_k \left(\frac{t_k}{1+t_k} \right)^2 \right], \tag{5.5}$$

where t_k is the AVE of the price gap for good k.

Price elasticities of consumer demand are not known. However, econometric estimates of the price elasticity of *import* demand are available from Kee, Nicita, and Olarreaga (2004) for all goods and products at the HS6 level. For prohibited products, estimates could not be obtained for Nigeria;[12] thus, we approximate missing elasticities by using data for the same products and comparable countries (neighboring ones at similar income levels).

In order to convert import demand elasticities into consumer demand elasticities, we need to subtract unknown supply elasticities. Under the assumption of less than perfect competition, we can assume that effective supply elasticities are less than unity. We fix them all at 0.5. Thus, demand elasticities are calculated as import demand elasticities minus one-half.

Overall, the welfare gain attributable to the elimination of prohibitions (and their replacement with tariffs equivalent to the ones applied on similar products)[13] is equivalent to an 8.5 percent increase in household real income. A breakdown of the increase in real income by income quartile is shown in figure 5.16: the mildly regressive character of the prohibitions shows up as a larger gain from their elimination in the first (lowest) quartile of the income distribution.

Real income gains are broken down by type of prohibited product in figure 5.17, which shows that a substantial chunk of those gains is generated by the elimination of import bans on household products, followed by textiles and clothing. This is true at every level of income.

Finally, gains in real income are broken down by region in figure 5.18. Gains are systematically higher in northern regions for two reasons: (a) the share of prohibited products in household income is slightly higher in the north, and (b) price gaps tend to be higher as well. That is, not only are absolute prices higher in those regions than in Lagos, but the difference between the price of

Figure 5.16 Gain in Real Income from the Elimination of Prohibitions in Nigeria, by Income Quartile

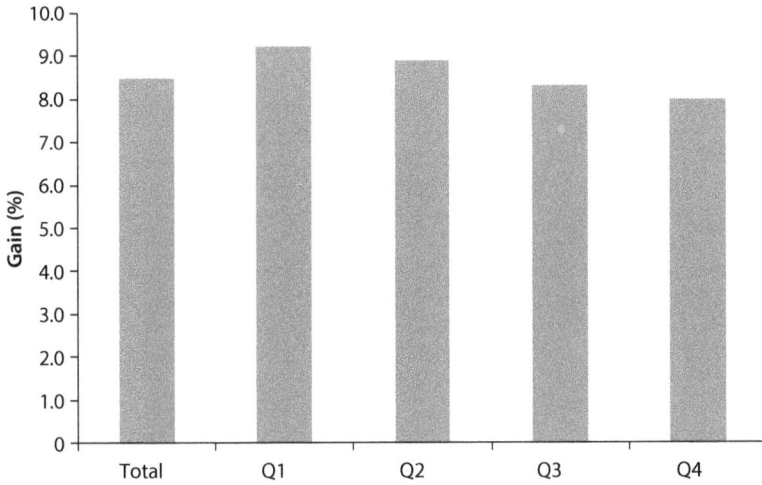

Figure 5.17 Gain in Real Income from the Elimination of Import Bans in Nigeria, by Income Quartile and Product Category

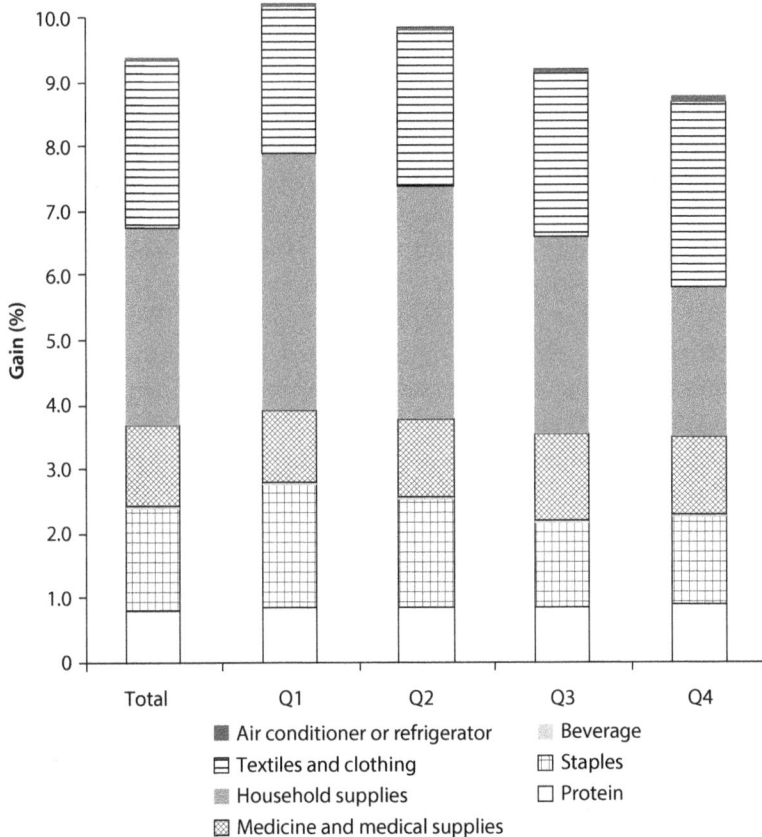

Figure 5.18 Gains in Real Income from the Elimination of Bans in Nigeria, by Region

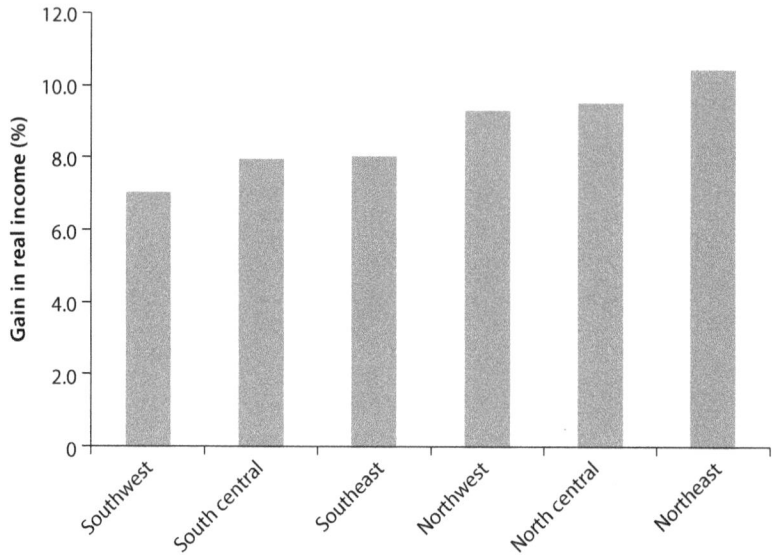

prohibited products and other products is higher as well. Thus, eliminating the bans benefits those regions more.

All in all, it appears that the elimination of import bans would have a pro-poor impact, both directly through differential impacts across the distribution of income and indirectly through differential impacts that favor the northern regions.

The effect on poverty can only be approximated, since Nigeria does not report poverty headcounts, Gini coefficients, or any other measure of the distribution of income included in the World Bank's annual *World Development Report*. Using household survey data to reconstruct these measures yields a poverty headcount ratio (US$1.25 per day poverty line) of 67.5 percent.[14] The change in real income induced by the phaseout of prohibitions, allocated by quartile of income distribution according to the estimates reported in figure 5.16, yields a poverty headcount ratio of 65.0 percent or a reduction of −2.48 percent. That is, given a population of 134 million inhabitants, about 3.3 million Nigerians would exit poverty, in real terms, as a result of eliminating the import prohibitions. To give a graphic rendering of the effect of the increase in real income involved, we blow up nominal individual income by the inverse of the price decrease and redraw the entire income distribution. The resulting rightward shift in the distribution is shown in figure 5.19.

The elimination of import bans would also reduce inflation through two effects:

- Reduce the price of banned products once the bans are lifted.
- Reduce the long-term inflation rate by switching products from high- to low-inflation categories because inflation is lower on imported products than on domestically produced ones.

Figure 5.19 Shift in the Distribution of Real Income Generated by the Elimination of Import Prohibitions in Nigeria

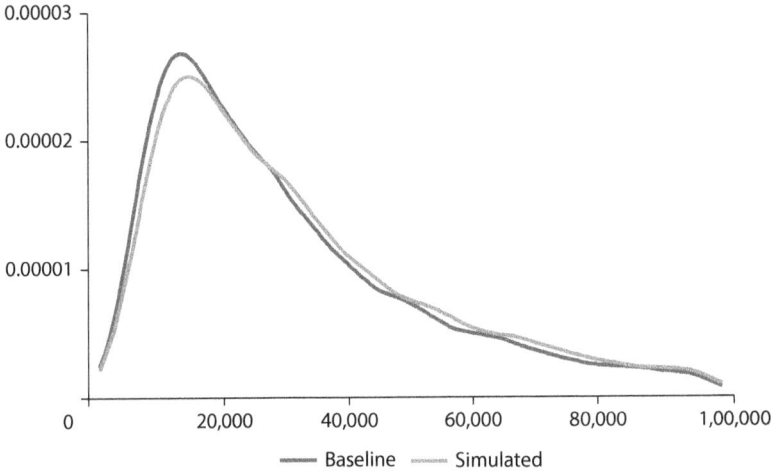

Table 5.8 Inflation Rates on Locally Produced, Imported, and Banned Products in Nigeria
Percentages

| Product | Local goods | Inflation rate | | Share of household consumption | Expected drop in price from the elimination of bans |
		Imported goods	Prohibited goods		
Staples	14.70	11.80	13.20	5.73	−20
Protein	15.90	8.80	17.10	6.23	−10
Beverages	16.20	8.10	13.10	0.64	
Household supplies	9.30	5.90	10.50	3.13	−50
Medicine and medical supplies		10.30	6.40	0.91	−60
Textiles and clothing			7.90	5.13	−45
Other imports		9.90			
Average on goods	14.00	9.10	11.40		
Lodging	18.30				
Utilities	22.20				

Table 5.8 shows the difference in inflation rates across these three categories of goods. Imports substantially slow down the rate of inflation, which is natural in a fixed exchange rate regime. The last column highlights the large price drop to be expected from the elimination of bans.

The effect on the consumer price index is illustrated in table 5.9 and in figure 5.20. Table 5.9 shows that, against a background of slowly decelerating inflation (from 11.9 percent in 2009 to 9.6 percent forecast in 2011), eliminating the import bans has a huge effect, quickly knocking a full 7.2 percentage points off the inflation rate; thereafter, the effect is more subdued, but still far from

Table 5.9 Effect of the Elimination of Prohibitions on the Price Index and Inflation in Nigeria, 2008–11

Indicator	2008	2009	2010	2011
Price index				
Baseline	100	111.9	123.8	135.7
With bans phased out	100	111.9	115.8	124.5
Inflation rate				
Baseline		11.9	10.6	9.6
With bans phased out		11.9	3.5	7.6

Figure 5.20 Consumer Price Index with and without the Elimination of Import Bans in Nigeria, 2008–11

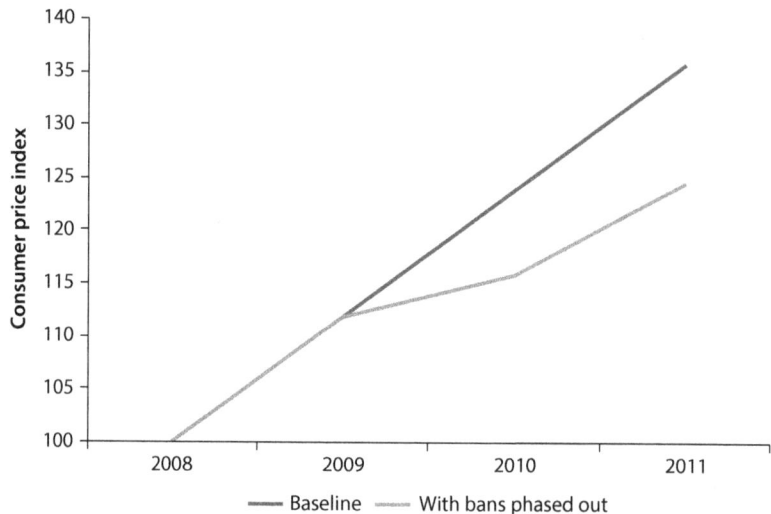

negligible (2 percent less than in the baseline scenario). This long-term effect confirms that import competition disciplines the market power of local producers, especially under a fixed exchange rate regime. Figure 5.20 drives the point home by showing the divergence in the path of the consumer price index with and without the phaseout of import bans.

Notes

1. The preliminary findings of this research were shared with the MoC at a national workshop organized in October 2014, leading to reforms that are addressing some of the problems identified in this section.

2. Rules of origin are the set of rules that must be followed to determine whether a product produced in Cambodia is eligible for preferential access into the importing country. For example, before 2011 the EU required any garment produced in Cambodia to undergo *double transformation* to be entitled to duty-free treatment. This meant that the garment had to be either assembled in Cambodia from woven fabric or knitted in Cambodia.

3. The EDD provides a comprehensive set of indicators computed from firm-level export data for 45 high-income and low- and middle-income countries between 2003 and 2009. For details, see Cebeci and others (2012).

4. These trends are common to most countries in the world and to most natural and social phenomena. The distribution of countries, cities, rivers, mountains, incomes, oil reserves in oil fields, and meteorite sizes has the same asymmetric pattern: few large specimens account for the bulk of the total but coexist with a high number of smaller, less important ones.

5. An Enterprise Survey is a firm-level survey of a representative sample of an economy's private sector. The surveys cover a broad range of business environment topics, including trade, access to finance, corruption, infrastructure, crime, competition, and performance measures. The survey indicates whether a firm is an exporter.

6. To estimate productivity, we use the 2009 standardized World Bank Enterprise Survey data. This information allows us to construct a pooled sample with information of manufacturing firms from our five countries: Cambodia (2011), Indonesia, Lao PDR, the Philippines, and Vietnam. We use two measures of total factor productivity. First, we compute the standard revenue-based labor productivity computed as sales per full-time worker. Second, we estimate the total multifactor productivity obtained as a residual from regressing sales on capital and labor. Each model estimates a log version of the Cobb-Douglas production function. Labor is computed as the total number of full-time employees, capital is the stock of fixed assets at the end of the previous fiscal year, and materials are the total annual cost of raw materials and intermediate goods used in production.

7. The only case where exporters do not have a productivity markup is in the case of total factor productivity in Indonesia.

8. Calculated according to the International Finance Corporation Doing Business methodology.

9. See http://www.wto.org/english/docs_e/legal_e/14-ag_02_e.htm#annV for details on the method of calculation.

10. Each product used in this average provides independent information on trade-cost differentials. There is no reason to weigh this information using consumption weights, as the relationship between trade costs and consumption volumes is unknown. Therefore, it is more appropriate to use a simple average than a consumption- or import-weighted average.

11. The EIU provides no information on the cost of living in Cotonou, which would have been a natural comparator for Lagos.

12. However, Nigerian customs report trade flows for prohibited products. Thus, Kee, Nicita, and Olarreaga's database does report some elasticities for those products, although only for a fraction of them.

13. As we are using the difference in prices between Lagos and Nairobi after excluding systematic price differences (for other similar nonbanned items) that are generated by trade costs and tariffs, the simulation implies that tariffs equivalent to those applied to similar but nonbanned items would be applied after the bans' elimination.

14. The only comparable (oil-producing) country in Sub-Saharan Africa with income-distribution data is the Republic of Congo, with a poverty headcount ratio of 54 percent at purchasing power parity. The Republic of Congo has significantly higher per capita GDP (US$1,782 in 2003, the year of Nigeria's household survey) than does Nigeria (US$502).

References

Augier, Patricia, Olivier Cadot, and Marion Dovis. 2013. "Imports and TFP at the Firm Level: The Role of Absorptive Capacity." *Canadian Journal of Economics* 46 (3): 956–81.

———. 2017. "Regulatory Harmonization, Profits, and Productivity: Firm-Level Evidence from Morocco." CEPR Discussion Paper DP11799, Centre for Economic Policy Research, London. SSRN: https://ssrn.com/abstract=2904321.

Cadot, Olivier, Mariem Malouche, and Sebastián Sáez. 2012. *Streamlining Non-Tariff Measures: A Toolkit for Policy Makers.* Washington, DC: World Bank.

Cebeci, Tolga, Ana M. Fernandes, Caroline Freund, and Martha Denisse Pierola. 2012. "Exporter Dynamics Database." Policy Research Working Paper 6229, World Bank, Washington, DC.

Elliott, M., Benjamin Golub, and Matthew Jackson. 2014. "Financial Networks and Contagion." *American Economic Review* 104 (10): 3115–53.

Kee, Hiau Looi, Alessandro Nicita, and Marcelo Olarreaga. 2004. "Import Demand Elasticities and Trade Distortions." Policy Research Working Paper 3452, World Bank, Washington, DC.

Melitz, Marc. 2003. "The Impact of Trade on Intra-Industry Reallocations and Aggregate Industry Productivity." *Econometrica* 71 (6): 1695–725.

CHAPTER 6

Conclusions

As tariffs have fallen worldwide and national regulations at the micro level have expanded, non-tariff measures (NTMs) have become more and more important. There continues to be demand for analysis of their effects, not only from countries seeking to engage in reform but also from countries seeking to understand the impact of the new mega-regional trade agreements such as the Trans-Pacific Partnership, Transatlantic Trade and investment Partnership, and Regional Comprehensive Economic Partnership. Such agreements have, or are likely to have, far-reaching provisions disciplining the use of NTMs, both of a horizontal nature—such as transparency and notification requirements—and of a sector-specific nature. Thus, assessing the impact of NTMs has become a high-profile topic for countries seeking to join mega-regional agreements, for those seeking to understand what they may be committing to, and for those outside those agreements but wanting to understand their impact.

This book has presented some cutting-edge methods for assessing the quantitative impact of NTMs. Despite a great deal of work to improve such methods, the precision by which such effects can be estimated has increased only modestly. Certain aspects of the problem are inherently intractable. Quality differences in products to be compared are still difficult to quantify, as are the various margins and markups occurring in international trade. Nonetheless, economists have gotten much better at "knowing what we don't know" about NTM effects. Older methods that focus on specific barriers have a strong foundation in economics and can produce more reliable results.

NTMs can have substantial impacts on household expenditures, on poverty, and on the operation of firms that participate in global or regional value chains. Even in the absence of precise measures, some NTMs clearly are not fit for purpose. If they are linked to domestic regulations, there are often clear ways to attain the same objective without unduly distorting international trade. Measures that affect trade more directly, as in the example of Nigeria's quantitative restrictions, have clear poverty and welfare costs. Analysis illustrating the impact of these measures can play a key role in creating the political will to streamline or reform such measures.

Sources for Policy Data on NTMs

There are two main categories of data on the incidence of non-tariff measure (NTM) policies: official data and data reported by firms or trading partners. Information reported by trading partners often originates from firms. Each type of information has advantages and disadvantages. Official data potentially reflect a wide inventory of the measures in place. However, they do not indicate which measures are likely to have the largest impact on trade. In particular, official data are not likely to disclose which measures are associated with administrative impediments, such as being slow, nontransparent, costly, unpredictable, or corrupt. Information arising from trader complaints is more likely to give at least a preliminary indication of what measures may cause the most concern for traders. At the same time, traders may potentially misunderstand or misrepresent the nature of the policies that they identify.

The most systematic attempt to collect information on official NTM policies are the United Nations Conference on Trade and Development (UNCTAD) data. These data assign each NTM to a particular classification (UNCTAD 2012), and the data are available online.[1] Table A.1 lists some of the countries for which data are available in the UNCTAD database. The data are collected by consultants who have been trained using a uniform methodology. However, different consultants may interpret the data collection template in different ways. In cases where specific policies are important, efforts should be made to verify the information independently. Another source of official data is notifications to the World Trade Organization (WTO) of trade-related measures, such as those under the sanitary and phytosanitary (SPS) and technical barriers to trade (TBT) agreements.

Data arising from trader complaints come from various sources. Several of these are from the WTO, which has developed the Specific Trade Concerns Database for SPS and TBT measures.[2] Concerns may also be raised in trade policy reviews, which the WTO periodically conducts for its members. The Global Trade Alert, organized by the Centre for Economic Policy Research,

See also the discussion in Ederington and Ruta (2016).

Table A.1 Countries Available in the United Nations Conference on Trade and Development Non-Tariff Measures Database as of 2014

Region	Code	Country name	Year of collection
Latin America	ARG	Argentina	2012
	BOL	Bolivia	2012
	BRA	Brazil	2012
	CHL	Chile	2012
	COL	Colombia	2012
	CRI	Costa Rica	2012
	ECU	Ecuador	2012
	GTM	Guatemala	2012
	MEX	Mexico	2012
	PER	Peru	2012
	PRY	Paraguay	2012
	VEN	Venezuela, RB	2012
	URY	Uruguay	2012
Africa	BDI	Burundi	2012
	BFA	Burkina Faso	2012
	CIV	Côte d'Ivoire	2012
	GIN	Guinea	2012
	KEN	Kenya	2011
	MDG	Madagascar	2011
	MUS	Mauritius	2011
	SEN	Senegal	2011
	TZA	Tanzania	2011
	UGA	Uganda	2011
	ZAF	South Africa	2011
Asia	BGD	Bangladesh	2012
	IND	India	2012
	LKA	Sri Lanka	2012
	NPL	Nepal	2012
	PAK	Pakistan	2012
	CHN	China	2012
	IDN	Indonesia	2009
	KHM	Cambodia	2011
	LAO	Lao PDR	2011
	PHL	Philippines	2010
Middle East and North Africa	EGY	Egypt, Arab Rep.	2011
	LBN	Lebanon	2011
	MAR	Morocco	2011
	SYR	Syrian Arab Republic	2011
	TUN	Tunisia	2011
High income	EU	European Union	2011
	JPN	Japan	2011

attempts to monitor new policy actions that may have a protectionist intent and originated during the global financial crisis. It has a time-series dimension and includes old measures that have been removed as well as new measures that have been imposed.

National governments often compile lists of trade-related concerns. In the United States, these lists take the form of the National Trade Estimate published by the Office of the United States Trade Representative (USTR). This comes in three volumes: one for SPS, one for TBT, and one for other measures. The European Union has an online Market Access Database. Eaton and others (2013) have assembled the CoRE NTM (Compilation of Reported NTMs) Database, which compiles recent measures appearing in the USTR's National Trade Estimate, the European Union's Market Access Database, Japan's Report on Compliance by Major Trading Partners, and the WTO's Trade Policy Reviews. The data, in Excel format, appear as an embedded file in the portable document format (PDF) file of the working paper describing them.[3] The International Trade Centre has conducted business surveys in various countries to identify non-tariff measures of particular concern both for exporters and for importers. The survey identifies not only the type of measure, but also the nature of the administrative obstacle that affects traders.[4]

Notes

1. The UNCTAD NTM data are available through the World Bank's World Integrated Trade Solution portal (http://wits.worldbank.org).

2. These data are available in Excel format at https://www.wto.org/english/res_e /publications_e/wtr12_dataset_e.htm.

3. See https://www.usitc.gov/publications/332/EC201301A.pdf. Opening the paper in Adobe Acrobat reveals a paper clip icon, which leads to the embedded Excel file.

4. See http://ntmsurvey.intracen.org/ntm-survey-data.

References

Eaton, Monica, Bradley Leatherbarrow, Zachary Shapiro, José Signoret, and Jessica Vila-Goulding. 2013. "The CoRe NTMs Database Version 2: A Compilation of Reported Non-Tariff Measures." Office of Economics Working Paper 2013-01A, USITC, Washington, DC, January.

Ederington, Josh, and Michele Ruta. 2016. "Non-Tariff Measures and the World Trading System." Policy Research Working Paper 7881, World Bank, Washington, DC, May.

UNCTAD (United Nations Conference on Trade and Development). 2012. *Classification of Non-Tariff Measures: February 2012 Version*. Geneva: UNCTAD.

APPENDIX B

Some Methods for Handicraft and Mass-Produced Handicraft Estimates of Tariff Equivalents

The basic strategy for a handicraft estimate of a single price gap is to compare a domestic price, which is considered to be distorted by the non-tariff measure (NTM), with a world price, which is assumed not to be distorted. Since these two prices are likely to be observed at different points of the supply chain, they need to be made comparable by adding and subtracting any margins for transaction costs, tariffs, or markups, so that the two prices are compared as if they were actually observed at the same point of the supply chain. Figure B.1 illustrates the way in which observed prices vary across a supply chain, which extends from the point of production in the exporting country to the point of consumer sale in the importing country.

The following formulas represent particular methods of implementing the general approach just described.

A reduced form for estimating the tariff equivalent ρ of an NTM is proposed in Linkins and Arce (2002), as adapted from Moroz and Brown (1987):

$$\rho = (P_d / P_w) - 1 + t + d, \tag{B.1}$$

where ρ represents the ad valorem equivalent (AVE) of the NTM, P_d represents the domestic (NTM-ridden) price net of wholesale and retail margins, P_w represents the world (nondistorted) price, net of wholesale and retail margins, t represents the ad valorem tariff, and d represents the ad valorem international transport margin. This represents a reduced form because some cost margins were removed from P_d and P_w prior to the calculation.

This appendix relies on material in Breaux and others (2014) and Ferrantino (2006, 2013), which can be consulted for further details.

Figure B.1 Prices along the Supply Chain

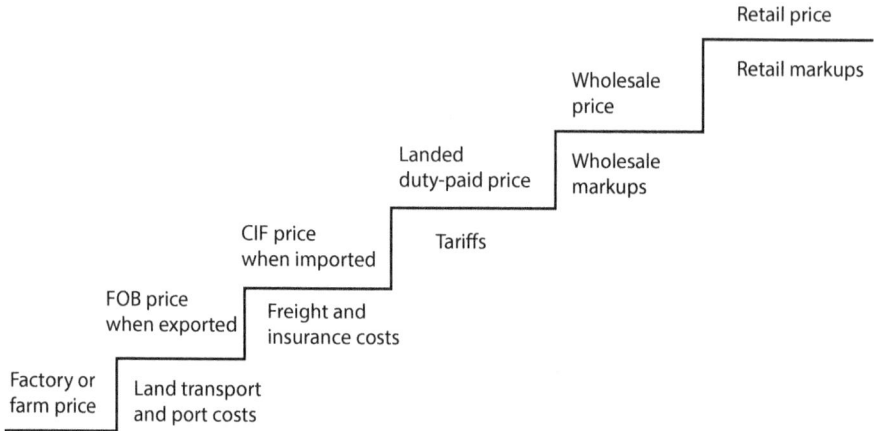

Source: Ferrantino 2013.
Note: FOB = free on board; CIF = cost, insurance, and freight.

An explicit representation of the set of margins illustrated in figure B.1 can be found in Ferrantino (2006), adapted from Deardorff and Stern (1997):

$$P_e = \text{ex-factory or ex-farm price} = MC + r_p, \quad\quad (B.2)$$

where MC is the factory marginal cost of production and r_p is the factory markup, which may or may not include some NTM rent.

$$P_f = \text{f.o.b. price} = P_e + c_x + r_s, \qu\quad\quad (B.3)$$

where c_x is the costs of transporting the good to the port and loading the ship, and r_s is any NTM rent earned by exporters.

$$P_c = \text{c.i.f. price} = P_f + c_i, \qu\quad\quad (B.4)$$

where $c_i = d / P_c$, the international insurance and freight margin expressed as a specific cost.

$$P_i = \text{landed-duty-paid or "in-country" price} = P_c + t_0 + r_m, \qu\quad (B.5)$$

where $t_0 = t * P_c$, import duties and para-tariffs are expressed as a specific value,[1] and r_m represents NTM rents accruing to the importer.

$$P_w = \text{wholesale price in the importing country} = P_i + c_w, \qu\quad (B.6)$$

where c_w represents the wholesale distribution margin, including any sales, value added tax, or excise taxes.

$$P_r = \text{retail price in the importing country} = P_w + c_r, \tag{B.7}$$

where c_r represents the retail distribution margin, including any sales, value added, or excise taxes.

The total effect of NTMs at all stages of the supply chain can be defined as

$$r = r_x + r_m + \theta r_p, \tag{B.8}$$

where θ represents the share, if any, of the ex-factory markup that is due to NTMs. The ad valorem equivalent of all NTMs is thus

$$P = (r / P_c). \tag{B.9}$$

The classification of NTMs adopted by Ederington and Ruta (2016) can be mapped into this framework. Ederington and Ruta group NTMs as *customs regulations, process regulations,* and *consumer regulations.* Customs regulations include quantitative restrictions on exports and imports and licensing and inspection requirements. Process regulations include labor standards, environmental regulations, and sanitary and phytosanitary policies, while consumer regulations include sales and excise taxes. In this framework, customs regulations are captured by r_x or r_m, depending on whether they fall on the exporter or the importer. Process regulations approximately correspond to θr_p. Consumer regulations correspond to those portions of c_w or c_r that represent taxation.

A mass-produced handicraft formula, which corrects NTM price gaps for multilateral differences in product quality, is found in Breaux and others (2014), adapted for the current notation:

$$\rho_i = \left(\frac{\Sigma \theta_{C,i} UV_{c,i}}{\Sigma \theta_{C,i} UV_{World,i}} \right) - 1 - \Sigma_i \theta_i (c_i)_{c,i}. \tag{B.10}$$

Here, the formula can be applied to all products i imported by a given country, for which the subscript is omitted in each case where an NTM is believed to exist. Thus, i denotes products, $\theta_{C,i}$ represents the import market share of source country C for product i, UV represents import unit values, and c_i represents the cost, insurance, and freight/free-on-board margin, so that the entire term represents an average transport margin for product i delivered to the country.

In practice, high-quality unit values should be used, such as those derived from national customs data or developed by the Centre d'Études Prospectives et d'Informations Internationales (CEPII).[2] Estimates of NTM effects are often an order of magnitude or more larger than those of the transport cost margin. Thus, for exploratory work, the final term can be dropped or assumed to be a small, uniform value such as 5 percent.

The formula of Breaux and others (2014) corrects for quality differences among suppliers, but not for quality preferences among buyers. In their paper, higher-income countries exhibited systematically larger estimates of the NTM price gap than lower-income countries. If applied to multiple importers, an additional step to correct for this income effect may be warranted.

Notes

1. This formulation assumed that the tariff is applied to the cost, insurance, and freight value, which is the most common practice. In the United States, the tariff is applied to the free-on-board value, and in Australia imports may be valued on either basis. In such cases, the formulas should be modified appropriately.

2. See http://www.cepii.fr/%5C/anglaisgraph/bdd/trade_unit_value.asp for the CEPII Trade Unit Value Database. These data are available from 2000 to 2010 for most countries and correct for the problem that different countries use different measures of unit value. When using unit values from World Integrated Trade Solutions, caution must be exercised because the United Nations Comtrade estimates quantities in some cases by assuming that all suppliers have the same unit value, subject to rounding error. Estimated quantities (unit values) are more frequent for manufactured than for agricultural goods. Users with direct access to Comtrade can obtain a dummy variable, indicating when quantities are estimated; otherwise, the data need to be inspected.

References

Breaux, Michele, Yasnanhia Cabral, José Signoret, and Michael J. Ferrantino. 2014. "Quality-Adjusted Estimates of NTM Price Gaps." Office of Economics Working Paper 2014-08B, U.S. International Trade Commission, Washington, DC, August.

Deardorff, Alan V., and Robert M. Stern. 1997. "Measurement of Non-Tariff Barriers." Economics Department Working Paper 179, OECD Publishing, Paris.

Ederington, Josh, and Michele Ruta. 2016. "Non-Tariff Measures and the World Trading System." Policy Research Working Paper 7881, World Bank, Washington, DC, May.

Ferrantino, Michael. 2006. "Quantifying the Trade and Economic Effects of Non-Tariff Measures." Trade Policy Working Paper 28, OECD Publishing, Paris.

———. 2013. "Using Supply-Chain Analysis to Examine the Costs of Non-Tariff Measures (NTMs) and the Benefits of Trade Facilitation." Staff Working Paper ERSD-2012-02, World Trade Organization, Geneva.

Linkins, Linda A., and Hugh M. Arce. 2002. "Estimating Tariff Equivalents of Non-Tariff Barriers." Office of Economics Working Paper 94-06-A (revised), U.S. International Trade Commission, Washington, DC.

Moroz, Andrew, and Stephen L. Brown. 1987. "Grant Support and Trade Preferences for Canadian Industries." Report for the Department of Finance, Department of External Affairs, and Department for Regional Industrial Expansion, Government of Canada, April.

Model to Estimate Trade Costs to Export

The analysis in the text employs information in the World Bank Enterprise Survey Database for Cambodia, Indonesia, the Lao People's Democratic Republic, the Philippines, and Vietnam. Data are for 2009 for all countries but Cambodia; its data are for 2011.

Using this database, we estimate a probit model explaining the decision of firms to start exporting.[1] We explain the probability of observing firm entry into international markets with measures of firm's size, experience, and foreign direct investment (FDI) status. Firm size is the total number of full-time employees.[2] The experience variable is the number of years that the firm has been active. Foreign direct investment status is a dummy variable that is equal to 1 if foreigners own more than 50 percent of the company. We estimate the model only for the manufacturing sector. We also use country fixed effects. The following is the preferred identification of the model:

$$Pr(entry_{fc} = 1) = \phi(\beta_1 small_{fc} + \beta_2 medium_{fc} + \beta_3 age_{fc} + \beta_4 age2_{fc} + \beta_5 FDI_{fc} + \gamma_c + \varepsilon_{fc}) \quad \text{(C.1)}$$

We use interaction terms between firm size variables and the Cambodia dummy to compare the ability of small (and medium) firms to export in Cambodia with respect to the average of the same type of firms in all other countries. We use these estimates to compute the expected probabilities to export by firm size, reported in figure 5.12 in the text. The regression results are presented in table C.1.

The fixed effect for Vietnam is absorbed by the constant of the model; therefore, all coefficients for the fixed effects of other countries are in relation to the Vietnam fixed effect. Intuitively, the fixed effects provide information on the impact of all unobservable variables at the country level that affect export status. Therefore, country-specific export costs are an important part of these estimates. In addition to the role of trade costs, these coefficients also capture many other country-specific factors that affect the ability of firms to export—for example,

Table C.1 Regression Results for the Expected Probability of Cambodia Firms to Export, by Firm Size

Variables	(1) exp	(2) exp	(3) exp	(4) exp	(5) exp
Total employment	0.446***				
	[0.019]				
Small (<20)		−1.517***	−1.605***	−1.522***	−1.582***
		[0.073]	[0.080]	[0.073]	[0.080]
Medium (20–99)		−0.910***	−0.910***	−0.846***	−0.864***
		[0.056]	[0.057]	[0.060]	[0.060]
Small * Cambodia FE			0.524***		0.356**
			[0.160]		[0.181]
Medium * Cambodia FE				−0.497***	−0.361**
				[0.158]	[0.170]
Age	0.003	0.007	0.006	0.007	0.006
	[0.007]	[0.007]	[0.007]	[0.007]	[0.007]
Age^2	−0.000	−0.000	−0.000	−0.000	−0.000
	[0.000]	[0.000]	[0.000]	[0.000]	[0.000]
FDI	0.807***	0.938***	0.957***	0.929***	0.945***
	[0.066]	[0.064]	[0.065]	[0.065]	[0.065]
Cambodia FE	−0.497***	−0.472***	−0.594***	−0.291***	−0.429***
	[0.091]	[0.085]	[0.090]	[0.105]	[0.122]
Indonesia FE	−0.233***	−0.256***	−0.238***	−0.252***	−0.240***
	[0.072]	[0.072]	[0.073]	[0.072]	[0.073]
Lao PDR FE	−0.351***	−0.427***	−0.425***	−0.426***	−0.426***
	[0.112]	[0.115]	[0.117]	[0.114]	[0.116]
Philippines FE	−0.083	−0.149**	−0.143**	−0.155**	−0.149**
	[0.071]	[0.071]	[0.071]	[0.070]	[0.071]
Constant	−2.720***	−0.228***	−0.206**	−0.255***	−0.233***
	[0.104]	[0.086]	[0.086]	[0.086]	[0.087]
Observations	4,963	4,976	4,976	4,976	4,976

Note: Robust standard errors are in parentheses. FE = fixed effect.
*** p < 0.01, ** p < 0.05, * p < 0.1.

the rule of law, level of education, skills, and others. This caveat is important to bear in mind when analyzing the results. The estimated fixed costs shown in figure 5.10 in chapter 5 come from the fixed effects estimated in specification 2.

We also employ iteration terms between firm sizes and the Cambodia country dummy to check whether the probability of small- and medium-size Cambodian firms to export differs statistically from the sample average across other countries within the same size of firms. The results are presented in specifications 3–6 in table C.1. We find that medium-size firms in Cambodia have a lower probability to export than the average for the same type of firm in other countries, while small firms have a higher probability.

Finally, for the scenarios of trade liberalization (trade cost reduction), we make within-sample predictions of the probability to export, by firm size, changing the coefficient of the Cambodia fixed effect to the average of all fixed effects (scenario 1) and to the Vietnamese fixed effect (scenario 2), using specification 3 in table C.1. These predictions are reported in table 5.4 in the text.

Notes

1. A firm is considered to be an exporter if it exports at least 5 percent of its total sales.
2. We use two types of size variables: (a) a continuous variable that is the count of workers and (b) three dummy variables by firm size.

Price Index of Products with and without Import Bans in Nigeria

Table D.1 Price Index of Products with Import Bans in Nigeria, by Region
Price index (national price = 100)

Item	Southwest	Southeast	South-central	North-central	Northwest	Northeast
Food items						
Palm oil	103	93	100	101	103	106
Vegetable oil	101	97	103	101	96	101
Margarine, blue band (1 tin)	100	103	106	106	94	94
Chicken, agriculture (1)	89	113	110	111	71	100
Egg, agriculture (1)	93	100	105	101	97	103
Beef, fresh boneless (1 kilogram)	97	100	110	100	93	99
Corned beef (1 tin)	101	105	104	96	96	100
Maltina-malt drink (1 bottle)	99	101	101	97	103	101
Average index	98	101	105	101	94	100
Nonfood frequent items						
Key soap (1)	95	107	104	104	94	99
Detergent (1 package)	102	101	106	98	95	100
Toilet paper	97	99	107	99	97	103
Panadol (1 package)	105	102	104	98	93	100
Iodine (15 milliliter bottle)	105	104	112	93	90	97
Average index	101	103	106	99	94	100
Textiles and clothing						
Khaht drill (100% cotton)	89	103	106	100	101	103
Ankara print	97	103	109	99	91	100
Polm (polyester)	93	115	101	96	96	103
George	106	90	87	107	91	117
Lace	104	98	99	110	83	108
Men's shoes	103	98	134	83	92	93
Women's shoes	96	105	129	93	89	92
Mattress (1)	96	94	100	97	102	110
Pillow (1)	103	95	100	98	99	106
Average index	99	100	107	98	94	104

Table D.2 Price Index of Products with and without Import Bans in Lagos, Nigeria
Price index (Nairobi = 100)

Without bans		With bans	
Item	*Price*	*Item*	*Price*
Staples		**Staples**	
Bread, white (1 kilogram)	471	Peanut or corn oil (1 liter)	353
Butter (500 grams)	140	Eggs (12)	157
Rice, white (1 kilogram)	303	Margarine (500 grams)	634
Flour, white (1 kilogram)	105	Spaghetti (1 kilogram)	82
Sugar, white (1 kilogram)	87		
Cheese, imported (500 grams)	102		
Corn flakes (375 grams)	116		
Yogurt, natural (150 grams)	75		
Milk, pasteurized (1 liter)	211		
Olive oil (1 liter)	171		
Potatoes (2 kilogram)	227		
Onions (1 kilogram)	225		
Mushrooms (1 kilogram)	125		
Peas (250 grams)	109		
Tomatoes (250 grams)	165		
Peaches (500 grams)	102		
Protein		**Protein**	
Fish, frozen (1 kilogram)	57	Beef, ground or minced (1 kilogram)	131
Fish, fresh (1 kilogram)	112	Lamb, stewing (1 kilogram)	119
		Pork, whole ham (1 kilogram)	121
		Chicken, frozen (1 kilogram)	124
		Chicken, fresh (1 kilogram)	150
Beverages		**Beverages**	
Instant coffee (125 grams)	188	Mineral water (1 liter)	94
Tea bags (25 bags)	58	Orange juice (1 liter)	93
Cocoa (250 grams)	77		
Coca-Cola (1 liter)	134		
Wine, common table (750 milliliters)	71		
Wine, fine quality (750 milliliters)	40		
Beer, local brand (1 liter)	140		
Beer, top quality (330 milliliters)	44		
Scotch whisky, 6 years old (700 milliliters)	40		
Gin, Gilbey's or equivalent (700 milliliters)	52		
Vermouth, Martini & Rossi (1 liter)	129		
Liqueur, Cointreau (700 milliliter)	29		

table continues next page

Table D.2 Price Index of Products with and without Import Bans in Lagos, Nigeria *(continued)*

Without bans		With bans	
Item	*Price*	*Item*	*Price*
Household supplies		*Household supplies*	
Light bulbs (2, 60 watts)	47	Soap (100 grams)	239
Batteries (2, size D/LR20)	192	Laundry detergent (3 liters)	300
Frying pan (Teflon or good equivalent)	130	Toilet tissue (2 rolls)	171
Electric toaster (for 2 slices)	85	Dishwashing liquid (750 milliliters)	109
Razor blades (5 pieces)	48	Insect killer spray (330 grams)	121
Toothpaste with fluoride (120 grams)	101	Aspirin (100 tablets)	296
Facial tissues (box of 100)	92		
Clothing		*Clothing*	
None		Business suit, 2-piece	124
		Business shirt, white	188
		Shoes, business wear	353
		Dress, ready to wear, daytime	353
		Shoes, town	297
		Shoes, dress wear	198
		Girl's dress	119
Other goods		*Other goods*	
Compact disc album	96	None	
Television, color (66 centimeters)	71		
Personal computer (64 megabytes)	66		
Kodak color film (36 exposures)	43		

www.ingramcontent.com/pod-product-compliance
Lightning Source LLC
Chambersburg PA
CBHW080426270326
41929CB00018B/3181